AN ILLUSTRATED GUIDE TO THE
ANCIENT MONUMENTS
MAINTAINED BY THE DEPARTMENT OF THE ENVIRONMENT
ON BEHALF OF THE SECRETARY OF STATE FOR WALES

Ancient Monuments of
WALES

PREHISTORY
by H. N. SAVORY, MA, D Phil. FSA

THE ROMAN OCCUPATION
by G. C. BOON, BA, FSA, FRNS

EARLY CHRISTIANITY AND THE EMERGENCE OF WALES
by C. A. RALEGH RADFORD, MA, D Litt, FSA, FBA, FR Hist. Soc.

THE MIDDLE AGES
by GLANMOR WILLIAMS, MA, D Litt. FR Hist. Soc.

THE INDUSTRIAL REVOLUTION
by D. MORGAN REES, MA, FSA

London

Her Majesty's Stationery Office

1973

Contents

Page   4   LIST OF ILLUSTRATIONS

5   PREFACE

7   PREHISTORY

7   The physical background

7   The first men

8   The first farming communities

9   Neolithic burial customs

11   Megalithic communal tombs

24   Henge monuments and standing stones

26   Hill-forts

30   THE ROMAN OCCUPATION

30   Military history

36   Forts

42   Minerals

43   Civil settlements

47   EARLY CHRISTIANITY AND THE EMERGENCE OF WALES

47   Early Christian inscriptions

48   The early Welsh Church

50   Holy wells

50   Sculptured crosses

52   The secular lordships

54   Hill-forts

55   Princely sites

55   Other dwellings

56   Linear earthworks

58   THE MIDDLE AGES

58   Historical survey

72   Castles

89   Bishops' palaces and other buildings

91   Monastic buildings

97   The disintegration and dissolution of the monasteries

100   THE INDUSTRIAL REVOLUTION

100   Ironmaking

102   Coalmining

102   Metalliferous mining

103   Slate quarrying

104   Roads, canals and railways

106   CONVERSION TABLE

107   FURTHER READING

113   NOTES

133   INDEX

Illustrations

Page 17   Pentre Ifan burial chamber
Barclodiad y Gawres burial chamber

25   Penrhos Feilw burial stones

39   Roman town wall, Caerwent
Roman amphitheatre, Caerleon

48   Margam Stones Museum

67   Dolbadarn Castle
Castell y Bere

74   Dolwyddelan Castle
Chepstow Castle

77   Tretower Castle
White Castle

80   Caerphilly Castle

83   Rhuddlan Castle

84   Conwy Castle
Harlech Castle

87   Caernarvon Castle
Beaumaris Castle

88   Raglan Castle
The Bishop's Palace, St David's

94   Tintern Abbey
Llanthony Priory

111   Castell Coch

Plans

Page 23   Fig. 1   Cairn plans: Bryn Celli Ddu, Tinkinswood and Pentre Ifan
31   Fig. 2   Roman Wales
37   Fig. 3   The Roman fort at Gelligaer
Distribution map showing location of guardianship monuments in Wales at end of guide

Preface

THE object of this guide is to help visitors to understand, and to enjoy, the Ancient Monuments of Wales—particularly those which are maintained by the State and so normally accessible to the public. The greater part of the text is devoted to an account of the monuments in chronological order, beginning with caves which, although natural in origin, were adapted to human use and ending with the comparatively complex man-made structures and machines surviving from the early days of the Industrial Revolution. Throughout the book the names of State-maintained monuments are given in italics (except where repetition makes this unnecessary) and at the back there is a list of such monuments, by counties, with a brief note on each.

As the guide is primarily concerned with monuments for which the State is directly responsible the balance of the text is somewhat distorted. The circumstances affecting guardianship, for example, favour the selection of compact sites rather than those covering many acres of useful agricultural land; the book therefore deals at greater length with burial chambers than with hill-forts. Similarly more space is devoted to monastic buildings in ruin than to cathedrals or churches in use because abandoned ecclesiastical buildings can be legally protected, whilst those in use cannot.

The guide differs from its predecessors (the previous guides to North Wales and South Wales) as the result of recent changes in the arrangements for the custody of Ancient Monuments in Britain. The Department of the Environment has absorbed the Ministry of Public Building and Works and the Secretary of State for Wales is now responsible for Welsh Ancient Monuments in the place of the Minister. Industrial Monuments have been included for the first time, since they now fall within the scope of the Ancient Monuments Acts.

The guide is not directly concerned with the two thousand or so 'scheduled monuments' in Wales which are also protected by the Acts but which remain in private ownership and cannot therefore be visited without the permission of the owners concerned. A list of such scheduled monuments is published separately by Her Majesty's Stationery Office.*

A Welsh language edition will be published in 1974.

---

*Not yet published.

Prehistory

by H. N. SAVORY, MA, DPhil., FSA

The physical background

In a general view, the land mass occupied by Wales, as historically defined, is marked off clearly enough from the adjoining parts of Britain by its character as an upland region, formed mainly of relatively ancient rocks and sharing many characteristics with parts of Scotland, northern England and the West Country, which together constitute the 'Highland Zone', stretching down the western side of Britain. The modern visitor, as he approaches it by road from any part of the English lowlands, is aware of a change to bolder but still well-wooded hills, beyond which high, bare moorlands soon come into sight, ultimately followed, especially in North Wales, by a hard core of rocky mountain land, the highest in southern Britain. He soon becomes aware, too, of the higher rainfall which, together with the tree-clearance which was begun by Neolithic man at least 5000 years ago, has meant that this has long been a land of stock-raising rather than cereal-growth. Here the farms are mostly small and were operated—at least in the western areas—until quite recently by the bearers of a distinctive peasant culture, economically poor, but rich in literary and musical as well as oral tradition, kept alive by a separate language which, in a sense, is Wales's chief ancient monument.

The first men

The oldest trace of human activity in Wales is a 'hand axe' of Acheulian type, made of quartzite from the South Wales coal measures, which was found on Penylan Hill on the outskirts of Cardiff. This primitive tool has been generally accepted as proof that man at least made fleeting visits to South Wales during the second interglacial period, perhaps as much as a quarter of a million years ago. It is, however, those caves which show evidence of occupation in later Palæolithic or Mesolithic times which represent the oldest human dwelling places and tombs in Wales which we can now identify; these are, of course, purely natural features, but in a sense they are monuments of the earliest human inhabitants of Wales and some are protected as such. The most famous is the 'Goat's Hole', Paviland (Gower), in which was found in addition to many stone tools of various Palæolithic cultures, a headless skeleton of a youth, ritually buried about 18 000 years ago (popularly and inaccurately known as the 'Red Lady' owing to the fact that the skeleton had been stained with red ochre).

After about 8000 BC, when the ice had retreated and plant life began to re-establish itself in Wales, the descendants of the Palæolithic hunters spread thinly over the whole country. Their Mesolithic flint tools have been found at many points along the sea-board but only rarely under the blanket peat of the interior uplands. Some of them may have come across the old land bridge from the Continent before this was finally severed, while others may have been driven northwards by the advance of the sea up the Bristol Channel, which by about 5000 years ago had left only a narrow ledge of marshy land beyond the present coast line where Mesolithic people could fish and fowl.

The first farming communities

By the end of the last Ice Age in temperate Europe, about 8000 BC, some primitive human communities in western Asia had already begun to domesticate plants and animals and to evolve a control over the food supply and the trade in rare commodities which was to lead within 2000 years to the first urban societies of the Near East. It was not, however, until some time after the beginning of the 4th millennium BC that the first Neolithic farming communities were established in the British Isles. These were small, purely rural communities which had arisen on both sides of the English Channel from the fusion of local Mesolithic hunters and immigrant cultivators from the south. Ireland and parts of western Britain seem to have been among the first areas to be settled, presumably because many of the earliest settlers came from the Atlantic sea-board of Europe. For this reason, it is not surprising to find that some kind of Neolithic settlement existed soon after the middle of the 4th millennium at Llandegai in Carnarvonshire, where later an important ceremonial earthwork, or 'henge' was built (page 21). But in Britain too, for many centuries after this, some local Mesolithic hunting and gathering communities maintained a separate existence, only gradually absorbing the arts of the newcomers. It is no doubt for this reason, as well as the influence of other continental Neolithic groups which had spread from central Europe into the Low Countries and northern France, that several distinct Neolithic cultural groups can be distinguished in Britain, from an early stage, by their styles of pottery and other features of their equipment, as well as by their burial customs. All, however, share the basic farming practices of cereal growing—wheat and barley, with flax occasionally added— and stock-raising, chiefly of oxen and pigs. The stone axe-heads with polished blades which were so important for their agriculture were soon being made of flint extracted from mines in the chalk regions of lowland England, or of various tough rocks which outcrop here and there in the Highland Zone. The factories where the latter were roughed out have been located at various places, notably at Craig Lwyd on Penmaen-mawr Mountain and on Mynydd Rhiw, near Aberdaron, in Caernarvonshire; there must have been several factories of this sort in north Pembrokeshire too, but these have not as yet been located.

Though by about 3000 BC several distinct cultural groups existed in Britain, there is little to show that their life was other than peaceful: throughout the Neolithic period the only earthworks constructed in Britain were for domestic and religious (not for military) purposes. Religion played an important part in their lives, and much of this revolved around a cult of the dead which produced their only permanent architecture: the 'cromlechs' which are such a prominent feature of Welsh prehistory.

Neolithic burial customs c.4000–2000 BC

IN all the peripheral areas of western and northern Europe where Neolithic cultures were strongly established at an early date there are abundant traces of the practice at this time of communal burial for members of the same family, clan, or social group, in chambers to which access would be gained periodically. Such chambers may be natural caves or artificial ones, dug in the rock, or they may be architecturally constructed, on the surface of the ground or in trenches dug into it, in either case with covering mounds of earth or stone. There is evidence for a good deal of variation in the actual burial practice, from successive burial of fresh corpses to reburial of decayed and more or less fragmentary skeletal remains, successively or on a special occasion when a number of individuals would be buried or reburied. The original home of this custom seems to have been around the shores of the Mediterranean, especially at its western end, and it is in southern and western Iberia and near the Mediterranean and Atlantic coasts of France that there are the largest and earliest concentrations of architecturally constructed communal tombs, including ones built in a 'megalithic' manner, with large upright stone slabs and large horizontal slabs used for roofing, as well as dry-stone walling and corbelling. Most probably the spread of such tombs to north-western and northern Europe was due to missionary contact rather than large-scale migration. In any case the great variety of forms encountered, and the great length of time —at least a thousand years—during which they were in use precludes any simple theory of introduction at one time, by a single folk movement.

There are a number of distinct regional groups of Neolithic communal tombs in the British Isles, corresponding to some extent to the cultural groups which are recognizable in other ways and which reflect varying continental contacts, or varying degrees of survival of the local Mesolithic population. One respect in which a large proportion of these tombs differ from the majority of continental sites is in the oblong or wedge-shaped covering mound, or cairn, which contrasts with the circular cairn which predominates in France and is universal in the Iberian peninsula. It is likely that the formative influence here is the tradition of house-construction followed by some of the parent communities on the Continent. Whereas around the Mediterranean the round house, sometimes built in a beehive form, became established at a very early date and survived until historic times in the Iberian peninsula (as in Britain), the Neolithic cultures of south-eastern and central Europe which did not themselves practise communal burial preferred houses of rectangular or trapezoid form. It is probable, therefore, that the long parallel-sided mounds that cover the earlier megalithic burial chambers of Scandinavia and parts of northern Germany are connected in some way with the long houses which were introduced into the earlier Neolithic cultures of this area from the south, and that the wedge-shaped earthen barrows of Poland and lowland England were inspired by the wedge-shaped houses of the Danubian Neolithic culture, examples of which have been found as far west as Holland and northern France. Certainly some Neolithic communities in Britain built oblong houses, with ridge-roofs carried on parallel rows of posts, and examples of these have been found in Wales at Newton Nottage, near Porthcawl, and Clegyr Boia near St David's. There can now be little doubt that this north European and British tradition of wedge-shaped mounds, which is known from radiocarbon datings to have been in existence at least from the middle of the 4th millennium BC, was in due course transmitted to groups in western Britain and Ireland which covered megalithic communal burial chambers with stony cairns.

When one comes to consider the origins of the various groups of burial chambers which are found in Neolithic barrows or cairns of any shape in the British Isles, one finds that here, too, house forms had an important influence. Recent excavations in earthen long mounds, both in lowland England and in the north European plain, have revealed traces of wooden 'mortuary chambers', usually of oblong, sometimes of trapezoid plan, in which lay the bones of large numbers of individuals in varying degrees of confusion. In some cases, the chambers had been burnt, apparently deliberately, charring some of the bones. These recent discoveries suggest that the megalithic chambers associated with long cairns in various parts of north-west Europe were inspired by what are presumed to be the primary wooden chambers of the North European plain, and this idea gains support from the fact that some of these chambers are trapezoid in plan. It is now clear, however, that the 'passage graves' of the Iberian peninsula and the Atlantic sea-board of France, with their circular or polygonal chambers and long entrance passages, also reflect the influence of the local house form, which in this case is circular, and includes beehive forms which could be the inspiration of dry-stone built burial chambers of this type. Although ritually burnt 'mortuary chambers' in long mounds, both in England and on the north European plain, have been similarly dated about the end of the 4th millennium, it is unlikely that the megalithic tradition in the British Isles can be traced back wholly, or even mainly, to the influence of timber structures. It is much more probable that Neolithic communities which alike in north-western and northern Europe owed a great deal to both the local Mesolithic groups and the central European Neolithic culture, adopted communal burial as a result of influences from south-western Europe, but chose to build various kinds of chamber and covering mound, partly as a result of differences in the building materials that were locally convenient and partly as a result of differing conceptions of the forms appropriate to the House of the Dead. The local Mesolithic element may have been responsible for deviations in ritual such as the burning of wooden chambers or the deliberate burning of actual corpses which appear in some British Neolithic groups, but are quite foreign to south-west European tradition of communal burial.

The Megalithic communal tombs of Wales c.3000–2000 BC

The Neolithic chambered cairns of Wales include examples of most of the main types of monument found in the British Isles, but so far none of the long cairns have been shown to have contained wooden chambers. This is understandable because most parts of Wales furnish suitable material for stone chambers. The long mound tradition is well represented, but two main groups have been recognized, one, in south-east and north-east Wales, which is closely related to the 'Cotswold-Severn' chambered long cairns of south-west England and another, in north-west and south-west Wales, which is closely related to the Irish groups of 'court cairns' and 'portal dolmens'. These two main groups seem to have been roughly contemporary and to have come into being early in the 3rd millennium BC; they follow a recurring pattern in Welsh prehistory, in which the country is divided between two spheres of influence, Irish and lowland British. There are three main concentrations of megalithic tombs of all types, in south-east, south-west and north-west Wales: other areas are poor in such tombs, partly for geological reasons, but partly, as must never be forgotten, because there always were communities in Neolithic Britain which did not practise communal burial of the kind we have been considering. At a later date, towards the middle of the 3rd millennium BC, north-west and south-east Wales were affected by a fresh cultural influence, which led to the construction of 'passage graves' with long entrance passages, megalithic chambers and circular covering mounds. These monuments derive ultimately from the great passage grave tradition of Iberia and Brittany, but they have special features which connect them particularly with the Irish passage graves of the 'Boyne' group and they represent a continuation of the westerly orientation of those parts of Wales in which they are found. All these types of tombs are scattered singly, or at most in pairs, about the countryside and represent the successive burials of small rural communities.

The Cotswold-Severn cairn

Four guardianship sites in Wales (*Tinkinswood, St Lythans, Parc le Breos* and *Capel Garmon*) share the characteristics of this English group, of which the heartland lay in the Cotswold Hills, although outliers are found in the chalk hills of Wessex as well as in the Welsh Marches. These cairns are wedge-shaped, though the 'horns' which flank the funnel-shaped 'forecourt' at the broad end are rounded in Welsh examples; their special characteristics, apart from the distinctive forecourt, are the prevalence of chambers that are approached by a short passage, the dry-stone walling used to supplement the large upright slabs and provide an even surface above them on which to rest the capstones as well as to revet the edges of the cairn, and the universal practice of inhumation, whether of fresh corpses or reburied ones. The long mound element is primary but the influence from the early south-west European passage grave culture is strong; even the later tendency, found in Breconshire and north Wales, to multiple, lateral chambers has analogies in the passage-grave culture of Brittany. The Welsh tombs of this group probably represent an initial influence on the coastlands of the Bristol Channel, as found at *Tinkinswood, St Lythans* and Penmaen (Glam.), and a later expansion from the northern Cotswolds into the central and northern Marches as far as *Capel Garmon* in Denbighshire. The orientation of these monuments varies considerably, but the forecourt and entrance end usually faces eastwards, with a variation in some cases towards the north-north-east or the south-south-west.

At *Tinkinswood* (Glam.) there is a large trapezoid chamber set at the north-eastern end of an almost parallel-sided cairn 130 ft long and 60 ft wide. It was excavated and partially restored in 1914 and as a result the dry-stone walling which contains the cairn can be seen, not only in the forecourt but at one point on the north side, where the probably deliberate 'extra-revetment' stones, which serve to buttress the walling, have been removed. The herringbone layout of part of this walling denotes complete reconstruction and it is doubtful whether the outer corners of the 'horns' were originally as sharp as they appear in the restoration.

The main chamber, 167 ft by 13 ft, is enclosed on three sides by upright slabs, but those which originally sealed the south side have been removed. The roof is formed by a single great capstone, estimated to weigh about 40 tons; like the other large stones in this monument it is made of a Triassic mudstone, quarried locally from a thin layer which out crops nearby. This chamber is approached from the forecourt through a short low passage framed with dry-stone walling and sealed by a slab which now lies outside. The remains found within had been badly disturbed at one time or another, possibly as early as Roman times. The bones which remained, however, represented at least fifty individuals, a large number for chambers of this kind. The grave-goods were, as usual, poor, but the pottery resembles that made in southern England in Middle Neolithic times, with the addition of some fragments of 'Bell Beaker' which suggest that the Copper Age newcomers of about 2000 BC re-opened the chamber, probably several centuries after its construction. Curious features in the body of the cairn are a series of transverse lines of upright slabs, near the south-western end, which appear to be purely structural in purpose, and a pit, halfway along the northern side, which is 10 ft wide and lined with dry-stone walling and upright slabs and may have had a ritual purpose, such as the exposure of corpses before reburial in the main chamber. Parts of a Neolithic pottery bowl found trodden into the surface of the forecourt may also have been connected with ritual.

At *St Lythans* near Tinkinswood there is a chamber which is now almost completely exposed and can be seen from the road, rising high above the eastern end of what little remains of a cairn about 90 ft long. It is much smaller than the Tinkinswood chamber but has the same trapezoid plan. As at Tinkinswood the single capstone, like the uprights, is of local Triassic mudstone. This monument has never been fully excavated, so that it is not known what evidence may still remain for the manner in which the chamber was originally sealed, or whether it originally had an entrance passage. Some time before 1875, however, human remains and prehistoric pottery now lost were noticed in earth lying outside the chamber.

At *Parc le Breos* (Gower) there is a small wedge-shaped cairn with rounded horns flanking a funnel-shaped forecourt and a double dry-stone revetment wall which cases the 'horns' and continues along the long sides to the truncated northern end. The chamber itself, however, is a passage grave with a pair of 'transepts', like those in some Cotswolds and Wiltshire monuments, approached directly from the forecourt at the south-eastern end of the cairn. It was first excavated in 1869 when it was found that no capstones remained but that the transeptal chambers were separated from the passage and in some cases subdivided by low sill-stones. Dry-stone walling was used to fill gaps between the upright slabs. The badly disarranged bones of at least twenty individuals were found in the various chambers but the only grave goods were two small fragments of Neolithic pottery. During recent re-excavation however, more pot-sherds were found on the surface of the forecourt under a layer of material which it was thought had been placed there to block the entrance after the last burial.

The best-preserved example in North Wales of the 'Severn' type of tomb is at *Capel Garmon* (Denb.) on some high ground overlooking the upper Conwy valley. The chamber consists of a passage, 15 ft long and about 4 ft high, leading from the southern side of the cairn to a rectangular ante-chamber with two bays, each of which leads through a gap narrowed by uprights forming jambs into a roughly circular chamber. The westernmost of these is still covered by a cap-stone, 14 ft by 11 ft, the only one surviving on the site. One inter-esting feature of the passage is the way in which the uprights are deliberately canted inwards as though to narrow the space to be roofed by corbelling and capstones and, perhaps, at the outer end, wholly by corbelling. Another is the unusual concave curve of the walls of the inner passage, which produces a bottle-shaped plan, recalling the passages of south Iberian rock-cut tombs of the 3rd millennium BC. The forecourt seems to have been deliberately filled in soon after its construction, and a similar blocking deposit had been placed in the mouth of the entrance passage, probably after the last burial. When the cairn was excavated in 1924 hardly any trace remained of the original burial deposits in the chamber, presumably because of disturbances which had begun centuries before. Some small fragments of Neolithic and Copper Age ('Beaker') pottery were, however found in the entrance passage. The latter probably represent re-opening of the chamber by the Beaker Folk about 1800 BC, several centuries after its original construction, and this may have been the occasion when traces of a fire were left at the north end of the entrance passage.

Irish Channel long cairns

In north-west and west Wales there are to be seen various types of chambered long cairn that seem to be related to monuments in northern Ireland and south-west Scotland and to be distinguished from cairns of the Cotswold-Severn group by certain characteristics which they share with some of the earthen long barrows of lowland England, which have now been shown to have covered wooden enclosures and mortuary chambers. The cairns of these Irish Channel monuments are usually wedge-shaped, though sometimes oblong; their forecourts are not funnel-shaped but concave, often enclosing half or more than half of a circle, and instead of the pure dry-stone walling of the Severn cairns are often lined with upright slabs which rise in height towards the chamber entrance, creating a more or less impressive façade; in general their kerbs are marked by blocks rather than the fine dry-stone walling of the Severn cairns. This concavity of the Irish Channel forecourts resembles that of the broad end of some lowland British long barrows where the place of upright stones was taken by vertical timbers bedded in a trench. Their chambers are generally rectangular and tend to develop into segmented galleries with two and even three or four compartments separated by transverse slabs or jambs. In northern Ireland there are two main types of 'court cairn' which may have independent origins—one with a deep forecourt and the other with an inner circular courtyard on to which one or more chambers open. A third type of long cairn, found chiefly in northern Ireland, has a single but often massive main chamber set in the broad end, with two particularly high up-rights at the entrance which tilt the capstone upwards towards this end and have a transverse slab between them which does not rise to the full height of the capstone. This arrangement constitutes what is often called a 'portal dolmen' and has usually been regarded as a decadent form of court cairn, but it is noticeable that monuments of this type in Wales are almost confined to the districts around the northern end of Cardigan Bay, while long galleries related to the segmented chambers of northern Ireland and south-west Scotland are almost confined to Anglesey and parts of west Wales. These exclusive distributions may mean that both types originated about the same time, and possibly quite early in the 3rd millennium BC.

All the Irish Channel long cairn groups, however, are linked to the lowland British long barrow tradition, not only by the forms of their chambers and forecourts but by the tendency to cremation. This had already appeared in some of the wooden chambered barrows of England by the beginning of the 3rd millennium, apparently at first in the form of deliberate burning of the chambers; but in the Irish Channel monuments cremation of the actual bodies appears to have been the usual, though not the universal practice. It seems that this development, which represents a break with the south-west European tradition of communal inhumation, may reflect the re-emergence of Mesolithic traditions in some British Neolithic communities which spread through North Wales and parts of Scotland to northern Ireland—along with the tradition of the chambered long cairns—while the builders of 'Severn' tombs adhered more closely to continental traditions. Nonetheless there are signs that 'Severn' traditions influenced the Irish Channel groups here and there and even spread to northern Scotland. Even in Anglesey there are several tombs, probably built late in the 3rd millennium, which seem to reflect this process.

The best preserved of an Anglesey group of wrecked long cairns with segmented galleries is to be seen at *Trefignath*, Holyhead. The gallery itself is now ruinous, but it probably once had four chambers, separated by transverse slabs rising almost to the full height of the capstones. It would have been 45 ft long, with the 'portal' at the eastern end represented by two exceptionally high, upright slabs set in line with the chambers. The first chamber going westwards is relatively well preserved; the second has been removed; the third has collapsed, and the fourth is now completely prostrate. There is now no trace of any forecourt or façade of uprights—or indeed of hardly any of the cairn—and the monument appears to differ considerably from typical Irish and Scottish monuments in its large size and the way in which the chambers are closed. As it has never been excavated it is difficult to be sure of its complete layout, but with certain other Welsh monuments it may be intermediate in the chain of evolution from English to Irish and Scottish long mounds.

The same type of monument may be represented at *Din Dryfol*. Here the gallery was aligned from east to west. At the eastern end the entrance, apparently about 6 ft wide, was flanked by two large upright slabs that may have been part of a large façade—in the manner of many Irish Channel cairns, including *Pentre Ifan* in Pembrokeshire (see below)—but there is no trace of this, and the existence of the northern upright is vouched for only by the discovery of its socket; the other upright still stands 10 ft high. Apart from this entrance feature only one segment of the gallery remains, at the western end, with a side-slab 11 ft long and 5 ft high still in position, suggesting that the overall length of the gallery was at least 48 ft. Excavations of this site have revealed cremated burials in the back chamber and traces of ritual offerings in the area of the entrance, which had evidently been sealed after the last burial with forecourt blocking material. At *Presaddfed* there is another wrecked monument with no trace of the covering cairn. There are two chambers, 7 ft apart, in line from north to south, and it is possible to interpret them as part of a segmented gallery from which the side-stones of one compartment have been removed.

The best Pembrokeshire example of an Irish Channel long cairn, and one of the best-known of all Welsh megalithic monuments, is *Pentre Ifan 'Cromlech'* near Nevern, which has long attracted attention by the height of its great capstone, under which it was possible for a man to ride on horseback, as various old pictures show. What remains at Pentre Ifan today is the mere skeleton of a single oblong chamber with a capstone 16½ ft long, which rests on a single upright

Pentre Ifan burial chamber
Barclodiad y Gawres burial chamber

at the northern end and is tilted upwards at the southern end over a
'portal' consisting of an H-shaped setting of uprights. The latter
stand at the centre of a curving façade of upright slabs which defines
a forecourt, rather less than semi-circular in plan and opening
southwards, at the southern end of the scanty remains of a wedge-
shaped cairn that must originally have been about 120 ft long:
restoration in recent years has shown up the outline of this cairn,
marked by the sockets of a line of small blocks which were once part
of the kerb. It is clear that the two pairs of large slabs which form
the forecourt façade, though now damaged on the west side,
descended in height outwards on either side of the 'portal'—in line,
no doubt, with the original surface of the cairn.

Excavations conducted at Pentre Ifan have shown that the chamber
stood in a large, roughly oval, pit which extended southwards into
the forecourt area but had there been filled in with stones piled
against the portal. The long sides of the chamber were found to have
been constructed originally of a mixture of dry-stone walling and
upright slabs; one of the latter can be seen lying on its side near the
north-west corner, and a modern stump fills the socket of another
near the south-west corner. It is naturally difficult to say whether
access was gained to the chamber in antiquity through this side walling or through a gap between the high blocking slab of the 'portal'
and its side slabs. No traces of the burials, presumed to have been
inhumations, had survived. The only offerings were a few fragments
of Neolithic pottery, of Irish affinity, from the pit just behind and
just in front of the 'portal', and some flints of no particular interest.
Pentre Ifan is, none the less, the best preserved of a small group of
Pembrokeshire sites which resemble the 'portal' dolmen group of
Irish Channel long cairns, and may have been built around the
middle of the 3rd millennium BC.

The best representative of the main Welsh group of 'portal' dolmens
adjoining the northern end of Cardigan Bay is at *Dyffryn Ardudwy*
near Harlech. There are, in fact, two separate chambers here, each
opening roughly eastwards up the slope of a hill, and standing on
the main axis of the remains of a wedge-shaped cairn about 100 ft
long. Excavation, however, revealed that the two chambers are not
of the same date. The smaller, western, one is a true 'portal dolmen'
with a high blocking slab set between two portal slabs that are
higher than the side slabs of the chamber and tilt the capstone upwards towards the portal. In front of the portal was a V-shaped
forecourt defined by low walls of laid slabs, the whole buried
under a small, squat, egg-shaped cairn, the material of which
was easily distinguishable from the remains of the wedge-shaped
cairn that was later thrown up over it, to cover the larger, trapezoid

chamber that was built later to the east of the 'portal dolmen'. The deposits in the two chambers had, as usual, been badly disturbed long ago when much of the cairn was removed for building material. The excavator, however, concluded that the burials had probably been inhumations, because no fragments of burnt bone from cremations were discovered, although these might have been expected to survive in the corners. The date of construction of the two chambers seems to be fixed in the early part of the 3rd millennium BC by sherds of fine bowls of Irish Middle Neolithic affinity found under their forecourt blocking material; other pottery of Late Neolithic and Copper Age types, found in the two chambers, seems to have been connected with secondary burials at a much later date, some of which at least involved cremation since fragments of burnt bone were found just inside the cross-slab of the larger chamber.

Passage graves

Wales has its share of monuments which carry on the great architectural tradition founded in south-western Europe in the 4th millennium BC and which involves a round or polygonal chamber approached by a passage leading in from the edge of a circular covering mound; a tradition which had its starting point in a local practice of building circular, beehive-shaped dwellings. That tradition is best represented, in the British Isles, by the numerous passage graves of the 'Boyne' group in central Ireland. Radiocarbon dates recently obtained at the most famous of these monuments, Newgrange, suggest that tombs of this kind were already being built before the middle of the 3rd millennium BC, but it still seems to be true that they represent a later phase of continental influence than that which produced the long cairns of the British Isles. The main part of this influence, it is clear, must have originated in the Iberian peninsula, but the complete culture which the Boyne tombs represent can in no way be attributed to a folk movement from south-west Europe, or even from Brittany, where the passage grave tradition is even stronger than in Ireland. The Boyne culture, in fact, was a composite one, the product of a special local evolution in the British Isles marked by a tendency to substitute cremation for inhumation and a fondness for the construction of places of assembly or religious ceremonial which can be grouped under the title 'Henge Monuments' (page 24), followed by influence from the south-west European passage grave builders. That influence impinged, to some degree independently, on the eastern side of the Channel, and as a result some fine passage graves were built in north-west Wales, and even where Liverpool now stands, as well as in Pembrokeshire. One of the two outstanding Welsh passage graves, *Bryn Celli Ddu*, has lately been shown to have been built on the site of a henge monument, one of several in North Wales which may be connected with the original movement from Britain to Ireland which established 'Secondary Neolithic' communities there.

The distinct character of the passage grave groups of the Irish Channel area is emphasized by the elaborate patterns, no doubt magical in purpose, which have been pecked with a stone tool on structural slabs. Certain elements in these patterns are certainly derived from south-west Europe and are connected with the 'Mother Goddess' cult which forms an enduring religious substratum in the Mediterranean area. But the spiral patterns which are so prominent in the Irish Channel repertoire are probably derived from its 'Secondary Neolithic' components, which had elements derived from central Europe, and may have been transmitted through perishable media—textiles, woodwork etc. Monuments of this group were commonly built on hill-tops and plateaux not on slopes and in hollows as was often the case with long cairns.

The two outstanding Welsh passage graves are in Anglesey, at *Barclodiad y Gawres* and *Bryn Celli Ddu*. The first of these (the Welsh name means 'The Apronful of the Giantess') originally consisted of a cairn about 90 ft in diameter, constructed partly of rubble and partly of turves, at the centre of which was a megalithic chamber approached from the north by a passage 20 ft long. After the excavation of this site in 1952–53, however, a concrete dome was erected over the chamber to protect its decorated slabs. At the time only one of the large capstones that originally covered the passage and the chamber itself remained in position. As in a number of Irish 'Boyne' tombs, the chamber itself is 'transepted' in a somewhat irregular manner, with small eastern and southern side-chambers (the latter entered over a sill-stone) and a larger western side-chamber with an annexe that was ritually blocked by means of several upright slabs which did not reach the full height of the roof at this point. In all three side-chambers fragments of burnt human bone were found, but the only grave goods were fragments of bone pins of the sort commonly found in 'Boyne' cremation deposits. In the centre of the chamber were traces of a hearth, in which a curious assortment of bones of small mammals, fish, reptiles and amphibians were found. In the southern side-chamber were found fragments of a cinerary urn of Early Bronze Age type, which must be related to a later use of the chamber or its covering cairn for burial. In the passage itself, in a recess at the inner end on the left-hand side, there is a free-standing pillar rather like two in the passage of the related Anglesey monument at *Bryn Celli Ddu* which recalls in a general way the cult pillars ('baetyls') near the entrance of passage graves in south-east Spain.

The most striking features at *Barclodiad y Gawres*, however, are the decorated slabs, which are clearly arranged in a significant relationship to the plan of the monument. As one passes from the passage into the chamber three decorated slabs are seen, two on the left and one on the right. The pecked linear patterns on these stones consist of grouped chevrons arranged horizontally and to a lesser extent vertically and incorporating concentric lozenges; the second slab on the left also has near the top a double-spiral pattern of the kind that is most characteristic of the Irish 'Boyne' tombs, and the left-hand slab also has a faint single spiral at the summit. All three designs are vaguely anthropomorphic and probably intended to represent deities presiding over the entrance of the chamber. In the case of *Barclodiad y Gawres*, however, the patterns have a particular relationship to ones that are carved or painted on the interior surface of slabs in certain passage graves of central Portugal. Further into the chamber, the back slabs of the east and west 'transepts' also carry scribings, consisting entirely of spirals. This is by far the most important assembly of megalithic art in Wales.

Bryn Celli Ddu ('The Mound in the Dark Grove') is the most impressive of all Welsh passage graves. It is now generally recognized that two separate and successive monuments occupied this site in the 3rd millennium BC: a henge and a megalithic communal tomb. The monument has been so restored that both these monuments can be seen, but it should be borne in mind that in order to leave exposed interesting structural features connected with the henge the large round cairn that formerly covered the passage has not been restored to its full circumference of at least 80 ft.

The henge monument was a circular enclosure, related to other sites in North Wales that are discussed elsewhere (page 24) and principally defined by a wide ditch, about 17 ft wide and over 6 ft deep, a section of which has been left open. The upcast from this ditch was probably used to form a bank on the outside, but owing to later developments on the site this has not survived. The ditch itself was 69 ft in diameter and would have had one or two entrance causeways. Within the enclosure was a circular setting of stone pillars, only two of which survive unbroken and are visible today. To judge by the evidence of the surviving sockets there were originally at least fourteen unevenly spaced pillars in this 'stone circle'— with a diameter of 60 ft—and some had cremated burials associated with them: the largest of the two that are still visible had the burnt bones of a child of eight to ten years placed near the foot. Such associations of cremation burials with henge monuments, with or without stone circles, are characteristic and occur, notably, at Stonehenge. All the displaced stones had either been removed from their sockets, or pushed over or broken up, apparently at one time, before the construction of the chambered cairn. This may mean that the builders of the latter were seizing and re-consecrating the holy place of a different social or tribal group.

The passage grave at *Bryn Celli Ddu* consists of a polygonal chamber 7–10 ft across and 6 ft high, approached from the north-east along a passage 27 ft long, only the inner part of which was roofed. The cairn which covered the chamber was revetted by a double kerb, bedded in the ditch of the henge and swinging in on either side of the outer passage. These two kerbs consist of upright slabs, particularly large near the entrance, surmounted in places by dry-stone walling. The visitor, on entering through the outer passage sees, outside the modern gate, two massive 'portal' slabs which have lost the capstone which they originally carried and then, on entering the inner passage, the low stone bench running along the right-hand side and the two small pillar stones, like the one at *Barclodiad y Gawres*, set in niches on the left. These features, like the large, free-standing pillar which stands inside the chamber, seem to relate to ones found in passage graves in southern Spain. A small spiral is carved about 4 ft above the ground on the first large stone on the left inside the chamber. The excavations showed that both inhumation and cremation has been practised on the site, and that at some stage in its use the outer passage had been deliberately blocked with stones and earth. A few flints and a stone bead are the only objects now surviving from the grave-goods. In the forecourt there were traces of interesting ritual—a small ox had been buried in a sub-rectangular enclosure, framed with stone and timber, a short distance outside the entrance (the spot is now indicated by small stones).

By far the most interesting ritual feature of the passage grave, however, was a pit found at the centre of the pre-existing stone circle, just beyond the chamber. This had had a fire lit within it, a human ear bone had been placed in it, and it had then been half-filled and a sealing slab placed inside. Above this a larger slab with an elaborate wavy pattern pecked over the two flat surfaces and the top, had been placed. A cast of this now stands close to the spot and the original is preserved in the National Museum of Wales. It seems that as part of their re-consecration ceremony the passage grave builders replaced some kind of central feature connected with the henge by a magic pillar, which was afterwards buried under the cairn. The fact that the magic pattern used in this case is particularly close to ones found in megalithic tombs in central Portugal may mean that the erection of the tomb at *Bryn Celli Ddu* was one of the first acts of an immigrant group which had gained spiritual authority over the henge-building communities of the Irish Channel area some time before the middle of the 3rd millennium BC.

? entrance

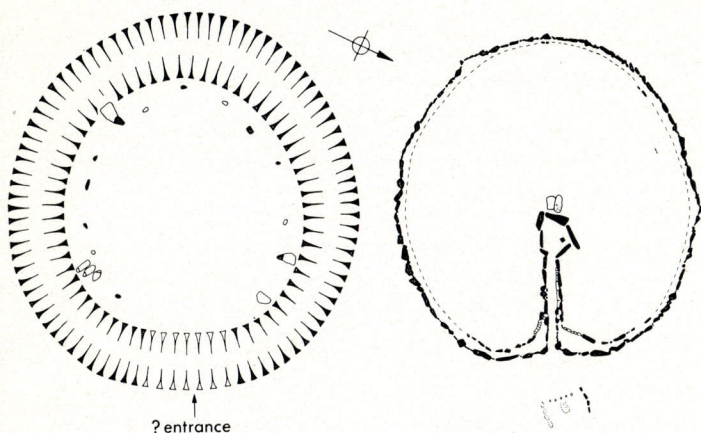

Period I: the henge monument   Period II: the passage grave

Bryn Celli Ddu, Anglesey

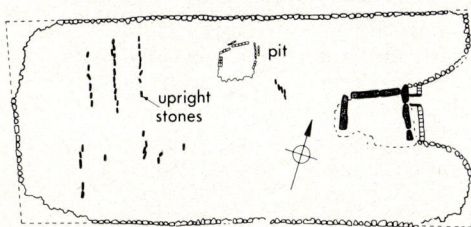

pit

upright stones

Tinkinswood, Glam. The chambered long cairn

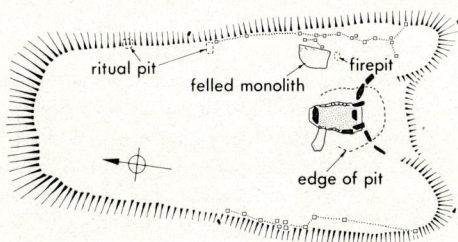

ritual pit

felled monolith   firepit

edge of pit

Pentre Ifan, Pemb. The chambered long cairn

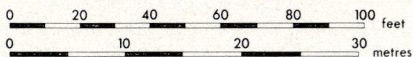

```
0    20    40    60    80    100 feet
0       10        20        30 metres
```

Fig. 1. Cairn plans: Bryn Celli Ddu, Tinkinswood and Pentre Ifan. Reproduced by permission of the National Museum of Wales.

Henge monuments and standing stones–
Neolithic and Bronze Age c.3000–1000 BC

The henge monument that preceded the passage grave at *Bryn Celli Ddu* has already been described (page 21), but this is only one of a number of monuments in Wales which take the form of enclosures rather than chambers covered by cairns and seem to have been primarily places of assembly for the living rather than houses of the dead, even though burials may be found in them, and the marked tendency of such burials to cremation links these monuments more with those particular communities in the British Neolithic which burnt their dead. Monuments of this kind were in use both in the Neolithic and the Bronze Age; though their best-known form involved the use of circles and other settings of standing stones— Stonehenge is the most complex monument of this kind—some sites consisted simply of earthworks with, at best, wooden structures within. Their precise function is not known, but it does not seem to have been military—quite often, though not invariably, the en-circling bank is outside the ditch—and it is generally assumed to have been ritual. This seems particularly likely in the case of *Stone-henge* and *Avebury*, but the precise nature of the ceremonial and its religious inspiration cannot be inferred from the archæological evidence. There is some reason for thinking that trade in stone implements may have been the special concern of the people who built some of the henges. Two large circles of this kind were explored recently near Llandegai in Caernarvonshire. One, dated by radio-carbon techniques to a period somewhat earlier than the middle of the 3rd millennium BC, had a single entrance and an external ditch, while the other, similarly dated to the early part of the 2nd millen-nium, had two entrances and an internal ditch. The earthwork known as *Castell Bryn-gwyn*, in Anglesey, seems to carry on the tradition of the second monument at Llandegai into the Early Bronze Age. On the other hand the stone circles which also carry on the henge tradition to an even later date in the Bronze Age on the Welsh uplands do not as a rule have prominent banks and ditches and are small and insignificant compared with Avebury and Stone-henge. The *Penrhos Feilw* stones near Holyhead appear to have stood originally near the centre of a small stone circle of this kind. Most Welsh standing stones however, like those at *Tŷ Mawr, Holy-head* and *Tregwehelydd, Bodedern*, seem always to have stood in isolation or in pairs. Here, again, the primary function seems to have been ritual, but burial deposits, usually cremations, are sometimes associated and such cult pillars, though originating in Neolithic practices, have mostly proved to be of Early Bronze Age date. They reflect the influence of the dominant newcomers of the earliest metal

age (*c.* 2000–1600 BC)—the 'Beaker Folk'—who played a leading part in introducing to Britain the custom of separate burial, of single bodies in pits or cists covered by round cairns, which eventually replace the Neolithic custom of communal burial. Round cairns or barrows covering Beaker inhumations or cremation burials of later date can be seen in abundance on the hills of most parts of Wales; many are shown on Ordnance Survey maps, but most prove on close inspection to have been badly damaged at one time or another and none has so far been taken into guardianship.

The earthwork at *Castell Bryn-gwyn* (Anglesey) certainly goes back to the early part of the 2nd millennium BC but its present appearance, that of a high and broad-based bank enclosing a roughly circular area about 180 ft in diameter, is the result of two reconstructions, the last of which seems to have taken place in the Early Middle Ages. In its first phase the earthwork was comparatively low, with a stone foundation, an external ditch, and an entrance close to the modern gateway on the west side. Its date was fixed by the sherds of late Neolithic 'Fengate' pottery found on its inner slope and the bronze awl sealed underneath it. Its construction is likely to have been related to the use of the stone circle and standing stones, surrounded by a bank with an internal ditch, that formerly existed nearby. Only

two of these stones now survive close to a field wall about a quarter
of a mile south-west of Castell Bryn-gwyn, one of them 13 ft and
the other 10 ft high. If these formed part of a stone about 40 ft in
diameter, as old accounts suggest, possibly with other settings of
large standing stones ('meini hirion') adjoining, there would have
been at Bryn-gwyn a religious centre as important as the one at
Llandegai in Caernarvonshire. The primary earthwork here may
have enclosed timber buildings either of domestic or of ceremonial
significance.

Hill Forts – Late Bronze Age and Early Iron Age c.1000 BC–AD 100

I T has long been quite clear, from the accounts of Greek and Roman
authors and from the personal and place names preserved by them
and by ancient inscriptions, that Wales, like the rest of Britain, had
been inhabited by Celts for some centuries before the Roman conquest. But when archæologists are asked to say (what the ancient
writers do not tell us) precisely when Britain began to be Celtic,
their answers vary, though few would regard the Early Bronze Age
builders of henge monuments as Celts. It does seem, however, that
about the end of the 2nd millennium BC some important changes
began in Britain, governed very largely by contacts across the English Channel. These changes affected technology long before iron
had replaced bronze. To judge by its equipment society was becoming markedly more warlike and the horse and horse-drawn vehicles
were now playing an important role in the service of a warrior class.
It is not surprising that evidence has lately been growing that the
practice of strongly fortifying settlements, which is so distinctive of
the Early Iron Age in Britain, really began in the Late Bronze Age,
as on the Continent. Thus about the end of the 2nd millennium BC
the building of earthworks for religious ceremonial was replaced by
their construction for purely secular purposes, perhaps because of
the influence of a newly-arrived ruling class. These early strongholds, especially on the Continent, usually took the form of coastal
or inland promontories defended on two or more sides by cliffs or
ravines and by earthworks or dry-stone walling on the side or sides
where approach was easier. It now seems that a number of forts of
this kind existed in the Welsh Marches before the end of the Bronze
Age, but there is no doubt that the great majority of the very
numerous prehistoric fortifications in Wales belong to the Early
Iron Age and the last five or six centuries before the Roman conquest. The Early Iron Age fortified enclosures of Wales show great
variety in size and methods of construction, according to their
function and the time at which they were built, and most of those

that have been scientifically excavated have been shown to have gone through several stages of development before they were finally abandoned. The Late Bronze Age promontory forts appear to have been commonly defended by earthern banks revetted back and front by timber palisades but by the beginning of the Iron Age proper in Wales, as in England, an elaborate tradition of dry-stone rampart building, with timber-framing used on a large scale, had been evolved. At first ramparts were usually single, with simple gateways, but soon lines of defence were multiplied and elaborate systems of defence at entrances—in which the approach to the gateway was narrowly controlled and commanded by bastions and towers, and the passage through the gateway itself in times of peace kept under surveillance by guard-chambers—were developed. These more elaborate hill-forts were mostly sited on isolated hills, with defences following the contours all round. At a late date, in the two or three centuries before the Roman conquest, a contrast is to be seen between a tradition of concentric, widely spaced banks, providing, no doubt, outer enclosures for the protection of cattle, found in parts of South Wales and the West Country, and one involving the use of closely sited, multiple ramparts each of which had a sloping front, not a vertical one like the earlier ramparts. The houses within these forts in Wales seem normally to have been round, in accordance with a native tradition established at the beginning of the Bronze Age, but houses of rectangular plan, more like those that had become more normal in most Celtic areas on the Continent, seem to be characteristic of some hill-forts in the Marches. Owing to their size, only a few Welsh hill-forts have so far been taken into guardianship, but one in Anglesey, *Caer y Tŵr*, near Holyhead, represents the conservative tradition of North Wales, and two in Monmouthshire (*Llanmelin* and the *Bulwarks*, *Chepstow*) illustrate the final stage of development, with closely-sited multiple ramparts.

Caer y Tŵr is a large hill-fort covering an area of about 17 acres on the highest part of Holyhead Mountain, but its defences are of a simple kind, apparently representing a single phase of construction. There is a single dry-stone rampart, built on the north and east sides at the top of steep slopes and using outcrops as natural bastions; but on the south-west sides the crags are so high that no defences were built and on the south-east sides it appears that any rampart that once existed has been removed for building field walls to the south of the mountain. The rampart takes the form of a wall which is 13 ft thick and up to 10 ft high when well preserved on the northern side; in the same area remains of a rampart walk to the rear, 4 ft wide and 3 ft to 4 ft high and with a breast-work 7 ft thick, can be seen. This type of structure, with battered revetment walls back and front and wall-walk, but no ditch in front, appears in several North Wales hill-forts and originates in the beginning of the Early Iron Age—in fact its origins can be traced back to the late Bronze Age on the Continent. The entrance at the north-east corner is recessed but otherwise of simple construction, without any sign of guard-chambers. A short length of rampart on the north side had been demolished, perhaps in antiquity. In the interior, at the summit (AD 720) are traces of an ancient lighthouse, and a round cairn of Bronze Age date; there are no signs of any huts contemporary with the fort and these, if they existed, were probably of timber. The large group of unenclosed hut-circles (*Holyhead Mountain hut-circles*) below the mountain to the south-west at *Tŷ Mawr*, which is known to have been occupied in the 3rd and 4th centuries AD was probably inhabited by the descendants of the prehistoric occupants of the hill-fort.

Llanmelin Wood Camp (Mon.) is a strong fort but encloses a comparatively small area—about 5 acres, which is much less than several other hill-forts in Monmouthshire—but with its defences and outlying earthworks it altogether covers more than 10 acres. It occupies the tip of a spur of Wentwood, overlooking from the east a small stream, but for most of its history at least, it was laid out as a contour fort with multiple ramparts and ditches continuing all round it without interruption: only on the north-west, owing to the steepness of the hill-side, are these defences reduced in strength. Thanks to excavations carried out in 1930–32 something is known about the history of the site, but most of the interior remains unexplored.

The main hill-fort had two phases of development. In the first the hill-fort proper had a strong inner rampart with revetment walls back and front and an outer bank and ditch with counterscarp, built as sloping fronted mounds; while in the second what had been a simple gateway on the south-west side of the site was strengthened by the addition of a dry-stone revetted inturn of the rampart on the south-east side thus, lengthening the corridor which led up to the gate and which could probably be commanded from parapet walks connected by a bridge over the gateway. At the same time a curious rectangular 'annexe', defended by banks and split into three compartments, was added to the south-east. It is possible, however, that before the first of these two phases of development a small enclosure existed on the site: all that now remains of this is a short length of curving bank and ditch projecting from the north-eastern defences of the main camp. The finds suggest that occupation of the main enclosure was concentrated in the areas immediately behind the rampart, though there may have been scattered huts, probably circular in plan, nearer the centre. The 'annexe' interior showed little

sign of occupation and was probably for cattle with a separate entrance at the south-eastern end. The inhabitants clearly lived mainly
by agriculture, though there is evidence for bronze and iron working.
The pottery from the first main phase of occupation resembles that
found in South Wales generally and in Gloucestershire and north
Somerset from the third to the first century BC while that associated
with the later phase continues the development down to the Roman
conquest; a small amount of pottery suggests sporadic occupation
of the site during the Roman period. The earthworks of the 'annexe'
gave shelter in the twelfth and thirteenth centuries AD to a small
medieval settlement represented by wall foundations. Further down
the hill, about 300 yards to the north-east, are the remains of a small
fortified enclosure which seems to have been a homestead occupied
at the same time as the main fort.

The culture represented at *Llanmelin* immediately before the Roman
conquest must be that of the Silures, the tribe which occupied south-
east Wales and fiercely resisted the Roman advance. It has sometimes been suggested that because Venta Silurum, the Roman town
built as a tribal capital, lies only a few miles away to the south at
Caerwent, Llanmelin may have been the tribal capital in the days of
independence; it is more likely, however, that the site of the Roman
town was chosen solely for its convenience on the military road from
the Sudbrook ferry to Caerleon and for its central position in the
best agricultural land of lower Gwent.

The Bulwarks Camp, *Chepstow*, is a small promontory hill-fort
standing on a plateau and abutting on a low cliff which here flanks
the river Wye on the west, close to its mouth. Originally it was
defended on the north-west, south-west and south-east by a double
bank and ditch, while it seems that the cliff always formed the main
defence on the north-east. Now, however, the banks on the south-
east side have largely disappeared. The area enclosed was about
$1\frac{1}{2}$ acres and the site must therefore be regarded as a strongly defended homestead rather than as a tribal stronghold like Llanmelin
Hill Camp. There is no superficial indication of an entrance and
this may have been along the edge of the cliff, on the north or south
side, and have been destroyed by erosion. The site has never been
excavated but the sloping-fronted multiple ramparts point to construction in the period immediately before the Roman conquest.

The Roman Occupation

by G. C. BOON, BA, FSA, FRNS

Military history

EXTANT Roman historiography relates little of Wales and nothing after 78, when completed conquest put an end to a generation of bloodshed. Archæology thus plays the chief part in the development of an historical perspective: but certainty in many matters is still elusive. The largest and most powerful Iron Age tribes were the Silures of the south and the Ordovices of the north, both with a stirring record of resistance to Roman aggression favoured initially by the mountainous character of their heartlands and subsequently by increasing Roman preoccupations elsewhere. The extent to which parts of Wales were under intermittent Roman control before 74, when the Governor, Frontinus, initiated the final conquest, is as yet obscure; but it is clear that Silurian raids on the periphery of the nascent province were responsible for the extension of the war into their own territory from late in 47, while a Roman raid against the Deceangli of Flintshire in 48 seems to have been intended to sever this tribe from the potentially troublesome Brigantes of the Pennine region. By 49 legionary forces were operating against the Silures, and within a year or two Caratacus, the Belgic king who had escaped from the initial British defeat on the Medway in 43, had been forced to transfer to Ordovician territory. Even after his famous last battle somewhere in Mid-Wales and his subsequent betrayal, the position remained unstable. The Silures defeated a legion in 52; the conquest of North Wales was postponed by Boudica's rising in distant Norfolk in 60; and as late as 78, on the verge of final subjection by Agricola, the Ordovices were able to exterminate a Roman cavalry regiment.

Archæological documentation of the pre-conquest phase has increased rapidly in recent years, and it now seems likely that the Roman frontier ran, by the 60's, from the Usk to the upper Severn and thence to the Dee, commanding thus all main lines of penetration into the interior, where advanced posts were probably maintained. One of the most important base-camps of the period was at Usk (Burrium), where excavations have revealed timber buildings of a very large establishment founded *c*. 60 on the site of a still earlier post. From bases such as this, or in the case of the south coast from estuarine bridgeheads, the Romans will have mounted their campaigns and punitive expeditions.

The natural lines of penetration are today the river-valleys, but in Roman times these were in general very heavily forested. It is not surprising, therefore, to find that such traces as there are of early Roman campaigns in Wales occur mostly in the uplands, where about a score of overnight (marching) camps are known. Even in these areas, however, conditions were far different from those of

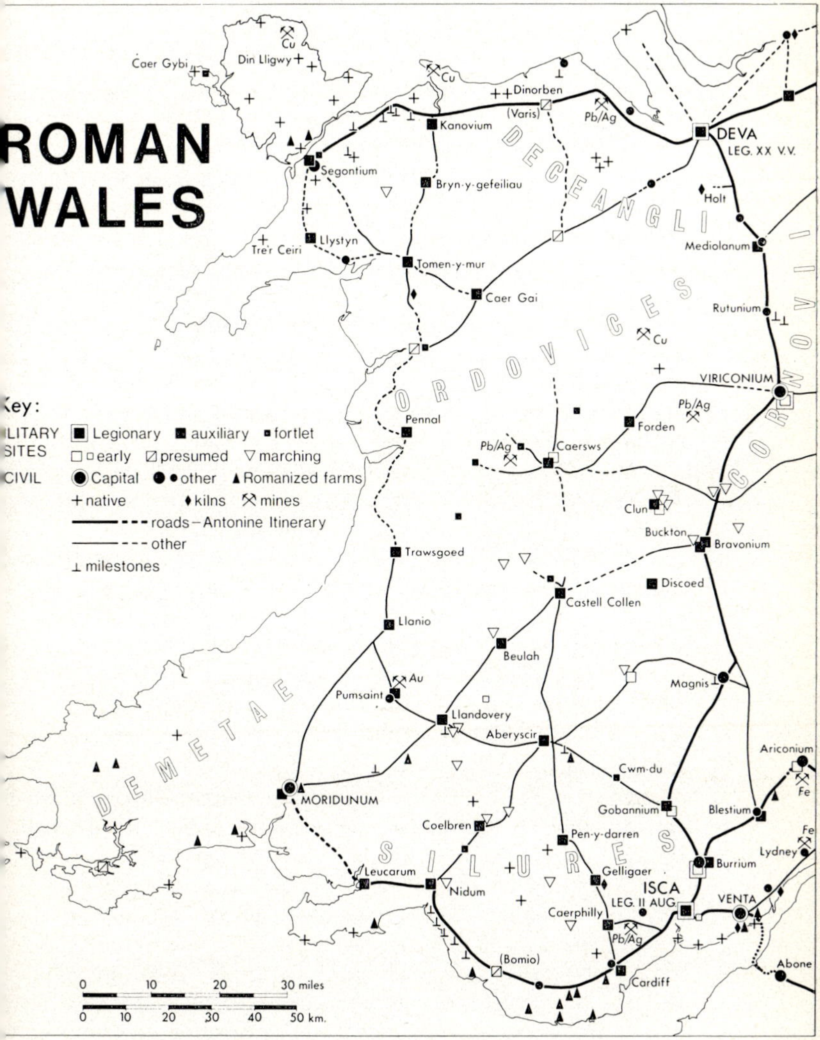

ROMAN WALES

Key:

MILITARY SITES
- ■ Legionary ■ auxiliary ▪ fortlet
- ▫ early ▨ presumed ▽ marching

CIVIL
- ● Capital ● other ▲ Romanized farms
- + native ◆ kilns ⚒ mines
- ▬▬▬ roads–Antonine Itinerary
- ------ other
- ⊥ milestones

Caer Gybi
Din Lligwy
Cu
Cu
Dinorben
(Varis)
Pb/Ag
DEVA LEG. XX V.V.
Kanovium
Segontium
Bryn-y-gefeiliau
Holt
Tre'r Ceiri
Llystyn
Mediolanum
Tomen-y-mur
Caer Gai
Rutunium
Cu
VIRICONIUM
Pennal
Pb/Ag
Forden
Pb/Ag
Caersws
Clun
Buckton
Bravonium
Trawsgoed
Castell Collen
Discoed
Llanio
Beulah
Magnis
Au
Pumsaint
Llandovery
Aberyscir
Cwm-du
Ariconium
Fe
MORIDUNUM
Coelbren
Gobannium
Blestium
Fe
Lydney
Leucarum
Nidum
Pen-y-darren
Gelligaer
Burrium
VENTA
ISCA LEG. II AUG.
Caerphilly
Abone
(Bomio)
Pb/Ag
Cardiff

DECEANGLI
ORDOVICES
CORNOVII
DEMETAE
SILURES

0   10   20   30 miles
0 10 20 30 40 50 km.

Fig. 2. Roman Wales. Reproduced by permission of the National
Museum of Wales.

today. Research into pollen-grains preserved in buried surfaces suggests that the mixed forest of oak and birch which had dominated the uplands since the Neolithic period still mantled large regions, but was now decaying under the influence of the wet climate. At Ystradfellte (Glam.) pollen-analysis showed that the 21-acre camp, large enough for a force of legionary size (5300 men), had been set in a cleared area, which slowly reverted to the natural state afterwards; but the heathy, grassy conditions now obtaining spread after the Roman period.*

The best-known marching-camps in Wales are at Y Pigwn ('The Beacon') at the summit of Trecastle Mountain (Brec.), though the site is not so easily accessible as that at Ystradfellte. At one time there was probably a clearing here; and the feebly-embanked remains of a 25½-acre camp overlie those of a 37½-acre predecessor, to show that substantial Roman forces twice marched this way, which in fact remained the route of the Brecon Gaer-Llandovery section of the Usk-Towy Roman road. In three of the four sides of each camp, entrances are visible, and take the characteristic form of inturned quadrants of earthwork ('claviculæ') facing the attacker's right-hand side. The ramparts, formed of upcast from a slight ditch, were never very much higher than today, but the soldiers carried stakes or used felled timber to make a palisade along the crest. Inside, they camped in regularly disposed heavy ridge-tents of leather, familiar from many a scene on Trajan's Column, and known to the troops as 'butterflies'. The only marching-camp at present identified in North Wales is at Penygwryd (Caerns.)

The map (Fig. 2) reveals in striking fashion the iron grip of Rome imposed in 74–78. At *Caerleon* (Isca) and at Chester (Deva) the two legionary bases, 50–60 acres in extent, lay at the roots of the Welsh peninsula. Coastwise and inland from each ran a series of lesser forts (3 to 8 acres), the knots in the network of roads, within a day's march of one another, controlling every estuary and valley-junction of importance, as well as the lonely upland roads, so that unimpeded passage of supplies was guaranteed and every native movement perceived. These forts were not garrisoned by legionaries (indeed the function of the legions was strategic rather than tactical), but were designed for the auxiliary regiments attached to the legions, and according to the situation held cavalry 'alae' of 500 cavalry troopers, or cohorts—some part-mounted—of 1000 or 500 infantry.

Second-century evidence throws some light on the division of Wales

---

*It is not perhaps generally realized that much of the surviving woodland was destroyed for fuel in the earliest phase of the industrial revolution. Thus there is now no wood at Gelligaer (Glam.), the 'Fort in the Woods' mentioned below.

between the two legions, probably on the basis of the territories of the two main tribes. The evidence comes in the form of tiles made in the legionary kilns* and bearing the appropriate stamp. Thus, tiles of the Second Augustan Legion, based at *Caerleon*, have been found at Usk, Abergavenny, *Brecon Gaer*, and Llandovery, while others of the Twentieth, based since 86 at Chester—the first legion there was the Second Adjutrix—have occurred at Cae'rhun (Kanovium), Caernarvon (*Segontium*) and Caersws in the Severn valley. Only four forts, however, have yielded inscriptions naming their garrison at any period, and we rely on the bronze citizenship-diplomas issued to retired auxiliary soldiers to fill out the picture. A diploma of AD 103, from Malpas in Cheshire, names four cavalry 'alae', one milliary and five quingenary (500 strong) part-mounted cohorts, one milliary cohort of foot, and four quingenary: they had been recruited in Spain, the Alps, Gaul, Belgium, Hungary and Thrace. One was the 'Ala Vettonum' from Spain, and since this regiment is known from an inscription to have been stationed at *Brecon Gaer* about the relevant time, it follows that all the others were in the Caerleon command. Other diplomas for 98 and 105, relating to the Chester command, reveal similar forces there; but the Twentieth also had responsibilities in the Western Pennines.

The army of occupation cannot well have been less than 20 000 men in addition to the legions, and their arrival in a largely forested region, whose inhabitants must mostly have lived at a bare subsistence-level, immediately produced logistical problems. An ordinary infantry cohort of 500, for example, will have required the annual harvest of 600 well-tilled acres if its grain-ration was to be met. A passage in Tacitus's *Life of Agricola* represents the Britons complaining because they were not only compelled to sell grain at a low fixed price to the army, but were also obliged to deliver it to 'remote and pathless places' and not to the nearest depots. The phrase must surely refer to the garrisons of the upland military zone about the year 80. That the arrangements were inadequate, even so, is suggested by a discovery at Caerleon, where a sackful of very mixed grain, diverted for brewing in one of the shanties of the civil settlement, caught fire on being malted, and thus preserved in charred state some weed-seeds of foreign origin, indicating importation from the Mediterranean.

The only real solution to the problem of supply was a reduction in the garrisons wherever possible—and by 100 the areas remaining dangerous (such as the Ordovician fastnesses of Snowdonia) and those where garrisons could be reduced or removed altogether (such

*The Twentieth Legion's kilns at Holt-on-Dee have been excavated. Those of the Second Augustan remain to be found.

as the south-west beyond Carmarthen, if ever in fact occupied) must have been discernible. By about that date, therefore, perhaps as many as six forts were given up as were five more under Hadrian. By the second half of the second century perhaps only fourteen or fifteen were still held, in some cases by reduced garrisons, as is shown in three different ways: (*a*) by the presence of bath-houses within the enclosure, as at *Segontium* and *Brecon Gaer*—the severely-limited space within the forts normally ensured that these large buildings were placed outside; (*b*) by reducing the original area enclosed as at Tomen-y-Mur (Mer.) under Hadrian and at Castell Collen near Llandrindod Wells (Rads.) in Severan times; and (*c*) by building a smaller fort adjacent to the original, as at Gelligaer (Glam.)* between AD 103 and 111.

Although it is known that the Second Augustan and Twentieth Legions joined the Sixth from York in the construction of Hadrian's Wall from 122, and of the Antonine Wall on the Forth-Clyde isthmus from 140, the degree to which the legions severally participated, and the calls made on the auxiliary garrisons of Wales for service in the new forts, are uncertain. Also uncertain is the effect which the removal of most of the British army to Gaul in 196–7 (when the Governor, Albinus, made his unsuccessful bid for the imperial throne) had upon Wales. It has been claimed that rebuilding at *Segontium* and *Caerleon* in the years following 198 indicates the repair of damage sustained at native hands during the absence of the troops, and this may be so: certainly the mid second-century stamped tiles from the Usk-Towy stations, the erection *c*. 160 of a large new fort at Leintwardine (Heref.) and perhaps also the apparent burning, *c*. 160, of the fort at Forden (Mont.) which protected the civil town of Wroxeter (Viriconium Cornoviorum), suggest that the army of occupation could not safely be reduced below a particular level.

On the other hand, it must be conceded that there is little unequivocal sign of destruction at the end of the second century as opposed to reconstruction—which might have become necessary for a variety of reasons—in the early third; and there is at present little reason to believe that all the forts occupied down to 196 were reoccupied in 198. Indeed the Severan pattern of occupation in Wales shows the Antonine dispositions reduced to the bare essentials. *Segontium* was held, as ever (though with a smaller garrison), perhaps in the main to protect the copper-mining industry of the Caernarvonshire seaboard and Anglesey: seven milestones from the

---

*Gelligaer is one of the classic military sites of the Roman Empire, providing a text-book example, in the Trajanic stone fort, of the accommodation required by a quingenary cohort of foot. Unfortunately, only the outline of the ramparts can be seen there today.

Chester road include five spaced throughout the period 198–268, besides one of Hadrian and another of Constantine; and *Segontium* is the terminus of one of the third-century *Antonine Itinerary* routes. Elsewhere, except at Forden and Leintwardine, which remained to cover the civil zone, the picture is less defined. Caersws and Castell Collen, though rebuilt, were not necessarily long occupied; and the same is true of *Brecon Gaer*. Along the south coast, little is known of military dispositions west of the legionary fortress, although it is just possible that the 'late' fort at Cardiff—the rebuilt enceinte of which is so striking a feature of the city centre—may have been erected, on the analogy of Reculver, as early as the first part of the third century against piratical raids from Ireland. Such raids would help to explain the evidence of legionary communication by sea with the remoter south-west, as deduced from the Prescelly slate ballast used to metal the third-century wharves explored at *Caerleon* in 1963; and also the repairs of the south coastal highway, where seven milestones, dating from about 240 to the fourth century, are known. This road, terminating at the tiny civil town of Carmarthen (Moridunum), is also listed in the *Antonine Itinerary*, which is sufficient to prove third-century official activity along it.

Later in the century, there is evidence that some forts were re-occupied, Gelligaer among them, although the character of the occupation is not always clear. *Brecon Gaer* is an interesting case, for here a crude late reconstruction of the defences, and a quarter of the coins discovered, seem to coincide with the remaking and maintenance of the Usk-Towy road from *c.* 260 to the fourth century, as five milestones again attest. In general it may be added that the majority of some 120 coin-hoards found in Wales belong to the later third and fourth centuries, and though this is a phenomenon by no means entirely Welsh, and one which may spring from more than a single cause, many hoards must have been buried because of the insecurity of the times, perhaps especially towards the close of the third century. It is likely that late Roman military dispositions, except at Forden and Leintwardine, were concerned more with external threats than with the possibility of tribal risings. Certainly, the army no longer retained its grip on the hinterland as of old. What happened at Chester is obscure, but excavations at *Caerleon* have recently shown that not only the great legionary hospital and baths, but also the headquarters, were dismantled before the end of the third century. Implicitly also, therefore, the legionary administration of all of southern Wales up to the Severn then disappeared.

What was now needed was a means of dealing with the Irish rovers. Although the inhabitants of a place such as *Caerwent*—the Romanized capital of the once-ferocious Silures—were safe enough behind

lofty fortifications, the raiders were able at will to pillage the countryside if warning could not be given. At Holyhead (*St Cybi's
churchyard*) in Anglesey, there survives some of the walling of what
seems to have been a late Roman fortified landing-place (although
all sign on the shore has long since perished). On the basis of the
plan, it is conjectured that the most likely date of its construction is
during the last great reorganization of the defences of Britain after
the barbarian attacks of 367–8. Holyhead may thus have been the
base of a small flotilla of scout-ships, perhaps camouflaged galleys
of the type mentioned by the historian, Vegetius. Advanced warning
could thus be conveyed of the descent of pirates on the North Wales
coast, where the regiment at *Segontium*, remaining until 383, could
take action. Other bases of this type may well have existed elsewhere
along the Welsh coast, particularly perhaps in the south-west; but
the most important of all was at Cardiff, where the late fort, of the
same general pattern as those erected on the south-east 'Saxon
Shore', must have been the headquarters of a Bristol Channel
flotilla. Deep-set in the Taff estuary, blind to the sea, it probably
received warning of hostile approach by signal from Penarth Head,
where a few late third century coins were found when St Augustine's
church was built in the last century. Very possibly the dedicator of a
mosaic floor in the late Roman temple at Lydney (Glos.), who was
the commandant of a naval depot, held a high position in this
flotilla.

It is interesting to see that some time after *c.* 335 *Caerwent* (*Venta
Silurum*) *town walls* were provided with external towers to enable
attackers to be enfiladed, and from Caerwent also comes evidence
of the same kind of Germanic soldier-settlers who were assigned for
the protection of many towns of Britain after *c.* 369. Parts of buckles,
etc., from their characteristic uniform equipment and lead-weighted,
barbed javelin-heads can be seen in the Caerwent collection at
Newport Museum. Coins from Caerwent continue after *c.* 383, the
general limit elsewhere in Wales, and include many thousands of the
little bronze issues of the House of Theodosius, the last to enter this
country in quantity from the continental mints of Gaul and Italy.
Other pieces in the collection, notably a fine penannular brooch of a
type known to have been in vogue as late as *c.* 500, suggest that urban
life of some sort persisted at Caerwent for much of the fifth century.

Forts

THE Roman army was methodical in all its ways. The sites of its
forts were laid out by means of a 'groma' or cross-staff set up in the
middle of the cleared area. The dimensions of the stone fort at
Gelligaer (Fig. 3) show that a standard measuring-staff of 10

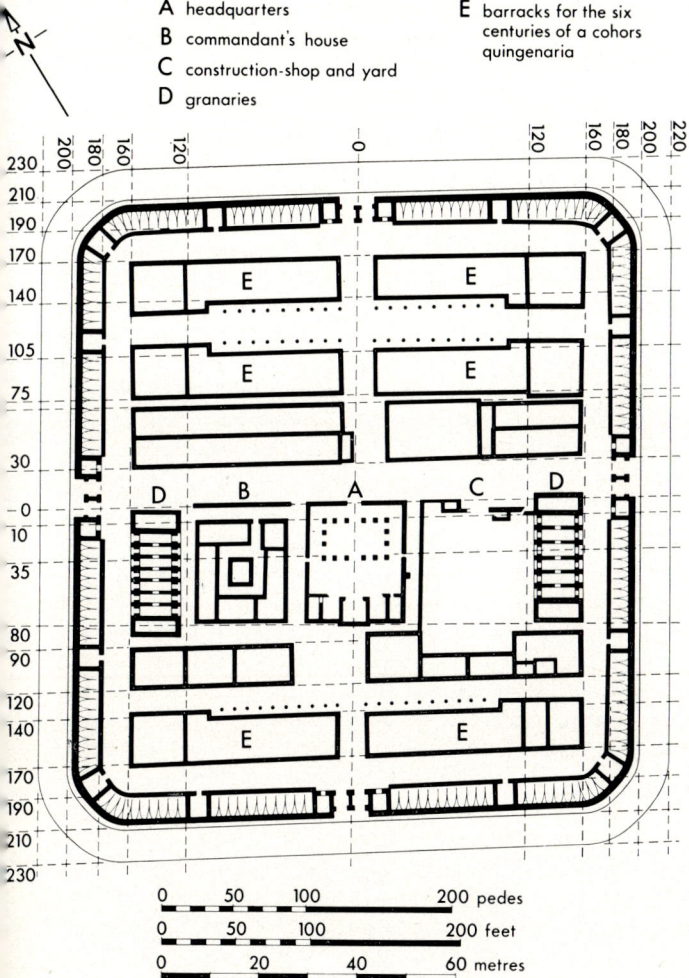

GELLIGAER (Glam.): Dimensions in Roman Feet (after Ward)

A headquarters
B commandant's house
C construction-shop and yard
D granaries

E barracks for the six centuries of a cohors quingenaria

Fig. 3. The Roman fort at Gelligaer. Reproduced by permission of the National Museum of Wales.

Roman feet (9.7 English) was employed in setting out the buildings. The rectangular area to be enclosed by the defences was closely related to the size of the garrison envisaged: thus a quingenary cohort of foot required about 3 acres, a cavalry 'ala' about 7½, and the legions, 5300 strong, a minimum of about 50 acres (as at Caerleon). Large or small, however, the same basic layout applied. The area was divided laterally into three by streets (the 'via principalis' between the side gates, and the 'via quintana' behind it and parallel). The central 'latera praetorii' contained the headquarters ('principia') and, in the case of auxiliary forts, this building was flanked by the commandant's house ('praetorium'), construction shop ('fabrica'), and a pair (usually) of granaries ('horrea') holding a two-year supply. The front and rear divisions ('praetentura', 'retentura') were bisected by streets leading to the other gates '(via praetoria', 'via decumana') and in the case of auxiliary forts were largely given up to barracks ('centuriae') and, where necessary, stabling. Something of these arrangements can be seen at *Segontium*, where the 'latera praetorii' and 'retentura' were consolidated and exposed to view many years ago—as is now thought, not altogether satisfactorily.

The headquarters can also be seen at Castell Collen, much overgrown from the excavations before the First World War. In a legionary fortress the arrangements were very much more extensive. The headquarters at Caerleon was flanked by barracks, notably for the milliary first cohort, and the commandant's house lay behind it, flanked by an exercise-hall and the quartermaster's work-depot. The 'retentura' contained barracks for four cohorts (six blocks, 240 ft long with centurion's quarters and twelve double cubicles for approximately 80 men). At *Prysg Field, Caerleon*, in the west corner of the fortress, one legionary barrack block is conserved—it is the only one to be seen in Europe at present—and three others are represented by 'ground-plans in stone' at the modern level. Another range for the remaining four cohorts of the legion was laid out at the far end of the 'praetentura'; and the space between these barracks and the 'via principalis' contained the great internal baths ('thermae'), the hospital ('valetudinarium'), and presumably six granaries ('horrea'), in addition to staff-officers' houses and other installations.

As first built, the forts, both legionary and auxiliary, were provided with a rampart of turf and clay derived from the broad ditch outside; the gateways, turrets, and the breastwork on the rampart were all of timber, as were the buildings of the interior, except at Caerleon where space was reserved for some of the more important administrative buildings, which were constructed in stone; and at Caerleon, too, many if not all the timber barracks were erected on cobble footings because of the dampness of the ground. The timber buildings

Roman town wall, Caerwent
Roman amphitheatre, Caerleon

were in general of a very massive construction. The framework of the walls was filled with wattle-and-daub, plastered and sometimes painted in colour; windows were glazed with thick, blue-green cast panes, and roofs were of heavy red tiles. Great care was taken to lay good streets and drains; the central sewers of the 'via principalis' and 'via praetoria' at Caerleon, dating from the earliest period of the fortress *c*. 75, were 6 ft high and 3 ft wide. Traces of a water-supply in 8-inch lead pipes—a gravity feed from somewhere to the north or north-west—have been found at Caerleon. The aqueducts at *Segontium*, known only from an inscription, will have been simple channels.

At varying dates in the second century, as the timberwork came to need extensive replacement, the opportunity was taken to rebuild the defences of various forts, and some of their internal buildings in stone; though often the stonework, in the latter case, still carried a half-timbered superstructure. The remains of gateways can be seen at *Segontium*, *Brecon Gaer*, and Neath, while at Chester one of the corner-turrets of the fortress is preserved at Newgate. At *Prysg Field*, *Caerleon* the defensive wall is not well-preserved, but the side and rear walls of two turrets can be seen, backed by large stone cook-houses erected about the middle of the second century. Some horse-shoe-shaped mounds at the back of the rampart are the bases of cooking-ovens of the late first century. Also to be noted here is the well-built latrine in the corner of the defences; it was flushed by water from a tank in the triangular lobby. A wall running across the centre of the latrine does not belong to it, but to one of a series of earlier rampart stores not now visible otherwise.

The late fort at Cardiff had only two entrances and, as can be seen at the north gate, the passage was narrow and recessed between two projecting towers. The half-octagonal towers for archers were solid except for the central ones on either side, where small sally-ports existed, at least on the east. The rebuilt enceinte gives a fair idea of what the original appearance of the fort must have been, but an internal gallery, seldom opened to the public, is false. The surviving Roman masonry is outlined in red stone at the foot of the walls.

Caerleon Amphitheatre (page 39), dating from about AD 80, is the only fully-excavated example in Britain. Its banks were never higher than they are today, the original metalled surface being found not far below the present turf. The outer wall was probably one storey high only, the entire superstructure of one, or perhaps two further storeys being timber-framed. The great uprights were probably set in the thickness of the outer wall opposite each of the buttresses or pilasters. Later, other buttresses, often very large—especially around the side towards the river—were added, presumably to support the masonry where weakened by the movement of the timber frame. An amphitheatre of this construction can be seen on Trajan's Column. At Caerleon, there was every intention to complete the building in stone, for all the entrances were originally vaulted; but the vaults were later taken down, except in one case.

A leaden plate bearing an inscription invoking the aid of Nemesis, goddess of fate, against a competitor on a chestnut horse was found in the arena, and suggests that beast-hunts on horseback were displayed there. The little chamber on the short axis, towards the fortress-wall, contains a niche which may have held the statuette of a deity. Another indication that an even grimmer type of contest was put on here is provided by a stone once set in one of the original buttresses, which shows the trident of a net-fighter ('retiarius').

The amphitheatre is very curiously placed, at an angle between a pre-existing bath-house (of which the furnace-room can still be seen) and the ditch of the fortress, half-filled to accommodate the amphitheatre in this space. There was very much less ground to the south-west than is now the case (excavations in 1963 showed that the Roman course of the Usk ran about a quarter of a mile nearer the fortress at its greatest divergence from the present channel) and this must explain the siting of the amphitheatre.

The principal finds from the numerous excavations at Caerleon are housed in the Legionary Museum near the church; it is a branch gallery of the National Museum of Wales.

Two other classes of military works remain to be considered. In addition to the auxiliary forts, a small number of fortlets or 'police posts' are known, as between Neath and Coelbren at Hirfynydd on the Neath-Brecon Gaer road, or at remote Cae Gaer (Mont.) in the foothills of Plynlimmon. Little is known of them. Another, established in a corner of the fort at Pen Llystyn (Caerns.), was about an acre in extent, had one gateway, and contained a number of sheds and perhaps living-quarters. It was not occupied for long.

The other class of work, in which Wales is unusually rich, consists of practice-camps, a hundred or two hundred feet square, having all the features, in miniature, of the marching-camps discussed earlier—rounded corners, and entrances defended by 'claviculae' or by traverses in front ('tituli'). The practice-camps mostly occur in groups, notably immediately south of Llandrindod Wells, where eighteen have been recorded, or near Tomen-y-Mur (five). The remains are very feeble, and it is essential to take a good plan if one intends to visit them. As their name suggests, they were built by auxiliaries on manoeuvres: as the Roman general Corbulo said, 'the enemy has to be conquered by means of the pick-axe'.

Minerals

'Pretium victoriae': the reward of victory—so Tacitus describes the 'gold, silver and other metals' to be found in Britain. Non-ferrous metal-production was naturally concentrated in the highland or military zone, and offset to some degree the costs of the occupation. The silver was extracted from lead, perhaps also from copper; and the Flintshire mines were active from the 60s, in the hands of a concessionnaire, and relapsed to private licensed production after a period around the middle 70s in government hands, when vast quantities of lead were needed for installations at Chester legionary fortress and the auxiliary forts under its control: a lead pipe in the Grosvenor Museum, Chester, dated to 79, bears the name of the most famous governor of Britain, Agricola. Production continued as late as the fourth and fifth centuries, as is shown by two late Roman coin-hoards, a late hoard of bronze vessels from the Halkyn Mountain, and perhaps by the remains of the massive lead sarcophagus of Camuloris found in Anglesey. In Shropshire the lead pigs are Hadrianic, and the exploitation may have been connected with the baths of the neighbouring town of Wroxeter. In South Wales there was desultory production at Machen, where a Roman mine-working, one of the very few well-attested examples in Britain, has been identified. The rich deposits of west Wales seem to have been little exploited. None of the British ores is very rich in silver, and the production of silver must have been somewhat slight in all the areas, compared with the vast quantities of ore extracted, much of which went to waste.

Copper-mining is attested in Anglesey and on the Caernarvonshire sea-board, mainly by bun-shaped ingots of metal, some stamped with the names of concessionnaires or bailiffs, and in one case with that of a company of entrepreneurs apparently based in Rome; copper-mines on the Great Orme near Llandudno also go back to the Roman period. Copper production at Llanymynech (Mont.) is also well-attested, and the workings there have recently yielded a small hoard of second-century silver denarii.

The most famous mine, indeed the only mine where substantial traces of ancient workings are to be seen, is the gold-mine at Dolaucothi, near Pumsaint (Carms.) on the Llandovery-Llanwrda-Lampeter road. The area now belongs to the National Trust. Most of the rock surfaces in two great opencasts have been defaced by the explosives used in intermittent periods of unsuccessful mining since gold was rediscovered there in the 1840s; but on the west side of the by-road to Caio a path through woodland leads shortly to two long, hand-cut adits, running almost level through the country rock to where there had obviously been a rich vein of auriferous quartz.

Perhaps even more interesting than the adits are the traces of the aqueducts or leats which descend the valley of the Cothi and the parallel valley of the Annell to bring water to the head of the mine, where it was used to flush away superficial and excavated debris and perhaps for various operations in the treatment of the ore. The most noticeable traces of the aqueduct systems near the mine are the reservoirs, several of which can be seen, as faintly-embanked platforms cut in the hill-side—particularly one on the east side of the Caio road, about 150 yds south of the opencast area.

This section may be closed with a general reference to the exploitation of coal outcrops in South Wales, and to the quarries for Caernarvonshire and Pembrokeshire slate. Nothing now remains of the workings, but the products, turning up in archæological deposits, testify to the keen eye which the Romans had for the natural resources of the countryside.

Civil settlements

Except as regards the purely Roman colonies, local affairs in Britain remained the responsibility—under the Governor—of the various tribes, whose administrations had been remodelled on the ordinary Roman municipal pattern. Towns were established at or near pre-Roman 'oppida' or else grew rapidly from the civil settlements of early forts. The Roman authorities hoped that an urban pattern of living would gradually impose itself, and in differing degrees such was the case throughout the lowland zone. By an edict of 212, all free-born provincials were accorded the Roman citizenship and thus became the political equals of the inhabitants of Italy; the local citizenship, however, was also retained. Wales and other parts of the highland zone, under a more or less severe military occupation, could obviously not participate to the same extent as lowland Britain in this Romanizing movement.

The Silures of the south are an interesting case. Long hostile as has been seen, they were the subject of a great Romanizing experiment made possible by the fact that their most fertile territory, along the southern seaboard, lay adjacent to the legionary fortress of *Caerleon*, whose 'territorium' had been carved from it. As early as the immediate post-conquest period, however, their little 44-acre town of *Caerwent* (Venta Silurum) came into existence, not improbably—though not certainly—on a site first occupied by an early Roman fort. The streets were laid out in grid-fashion on either side of the main London, Caerleon and West Wales road; like the headquarters of a legionary fortress—and very like it in plan—the 'forum' (market-place) and adjoining 'basilica' (assembly-hall, with council-chamber and offices) stood centrally on the north side of this street, and opposite lay the main public baths; adjacent lay an important *temple* in its own sacred enclosure—apart from the remains of two houses on the *Pound Lane* site further west, the only Roman building now exposed. Houses great and small, the best of them built round court-yards, many having mosaic floors, hypocaust heating, and walls as gaily or elegantly painted as any in Britain, have been uncovered in excavations; some sixty excavated buildings form perhaps half the total. Several shops, some where minor manufacturing processes were carried on, have also been explored but the excavations mainly took place before the First World War and the chronological picture of the development and decline of Venta is as yet indistinct.

The largest houses were clearly the residences of the tribal notables who composed the 'ordo' or council mentioned on an inscribed statue-pedestal now preserved in the porch of St Stephen's church; it commemorates a patron of the tribe, a former commander of the neighbouring Legion, and dates shortly before 220. The 'respublica civitatis Silurum' of the last two lines of the text is an expression paralleled elsewhere. It probably refers to all the inhabitants of the tribal area, countryfolk and townsfolk alike: 'the Commonwealth of the Community of the Silures'. The *town-wall* is among the best preserved in Britain, and has a series of hollow multi-angular towers for archers on the north and south sides. These date from about the middle of the fourth century, and may be a local imitation of the towers of Cardiff fort. The stone wall to which they were added may not be very much earlier. The visitor will notice that both the south and north gates have been blocked at some late Roman date—the one completely, the other to leave a low sally-port. Little remains of the east and west gates, which had double passageways and towers.

The southern coastal fringe was extensively developed in Roman times. The sites of numerous farmsteads (villas, where a fairly advanced agriculture was practised) are known and several have been excavated, notably at Llantwit Major (Glam.) and Whitton Cross-roads (Glam.), the latter on the site of an Iron Age homestead. No remains, however, are exposed to view. At Caldicot not far from Caerwent,* there were potteries in the third century, and at a superb site high above the Wye at Chepstow—the Wyndcliff—there was probably a rural temple, as again at St Donats on the Glamorgan-shire coast. The Vale of Usk was also exploited agriculturally, as the partly-explored site of a rich villa at Llanfrynach, near Brecon, suggests; but, on the other hand, the uplands forming much of the tribal area remained primitive. There is little sign of Romanized life; the

---

*Caerwent has produced a pewter bowl bearing a scratched Christian monogram, the only definite evidence of Christianity in Roman Wales. It is in Newport Museum.

inhabitants clung to the old ways. Among sites of the period are hut-groups above Ystrad Rhondda, Blaen Rhondda, and Aberdare, but little is known of them. A cave in Glyntawe seems to have been the burial-place of such communities as these, yielding fine brooches from an otherwise impoverished assemblage of material. Some forty individuals were interred there, at a time when cremation was the civilized rite in the lowlands.

West of the Silures lay the Demetae of Carmarthenshire and Pembrokeshire. Recent excavations have shown that their town of Moridunum was a little walled place of some 15 acres, which seems to have developed from the civil settlement of an early fort. Though Moridunum is nowhere in our sources given the tribal appellation which distinguishes Caerwent and various other towns in Britain as capitals, and although the geographer Ptolemy also lists Loventinum —Dolaucothi?—as a 'polis' of this tribe, it would be idle to deny Carmarthen the *de facto* status of Demetian administrative centre. Various Romanized farms are known in the tribal territory, notably at Cwmbrwyn, a single block about 100 ft long within a half-acre ditched-and-banked enclosure, and at Llys Brychan, Llangadog in the Towy valley; a mosaic has been recorded as far west as the Western Cleddau. Here and there, Iron Age hillforts remained in occasional occupation, and Coygan Camp near Laugharne is the most important excavated example. Around the years 270–300 a rectangular dry-stone building and three sheds, together forming a little farmstead, existed within the old ramparts. One of the interesting discoveries here was a hoard of tiny counterfeit coins which had been produced on the spot *c.* 282.

The territory of the Cornovii of the central and northern borderland extended some distance up the Severn valley from the capital of Wroxeter; and at Welshpool the burial or cenotaph of some country notable of the second century was discovered during alterations to the cattle-market. Objects associated included fine Roman bronze vessels of the first century (notably a unique ewer having a handle modelled in the form of the young Dionysus) a yew-wood pail with one surviving handle-escutcheon in the form of a bronze ox-head of late Celtic design and native ironwork—fire-dog and lamp-standards —of some distinction.

Coming finally to the territory of the Ordovices, Ptolemy again gives them two towns, Mediolanum and Brannogenium. Of these, the first may be Caersws, where there was a large civil settlement; the other is unknown. The tribe, however, was little Romanized, and there was certainly no civil town of any consequence in its territory: a bath-house at Tremadoc, apparently isolated, could mark the provision of normal urban facilities without, as it were, a town to go with them:

in this case a place of assembly, licensed by the Roman authorities, would have been the most important. The majestic hill-forts which crown many a summit of the north-west were perhaps the nearest Ordovician approach to nucleated settlement, the best example being at Tre'r Ceiri (Caerns.) in Lleyn: numerous hut-circles appear here, and there was a fourth-century occupation; but this knew not the use of coins, and the contrast with the excavated site of Dinorben (Denbs.) is complete. A fairly well-to do farmstead existed at Dinorben in the later third and fourth centuries, yielding some 250 coins—a respectable total even for a villa of the lowland zone—and possibly derived from the sale of produce to the garrison of *Segontium* until 353, when the series virtually stops.

Perhaps the most characteristic civil remains of the Roman period (though all do not belong to it) in North Wales are the primitive homesteads known by the traditional name of 'cytiau'r Gwyddelod' ('Irishmen's houses'). They dot the sea-facing slopes between the Dyfi and the Clwyd, and appear also in Anglesey, where there is the best-known of all, *Din Lligwy*. This farmstead or settlement consists of a kite-shaped enclosure some 200 ft across, with various circular or sub-rectangular buildings within, mostly attached to the wall of massive stones; occupation continued from the second to the fourth centuries. Not all 'cytiau' are of this distinction; those at Holyhead (*Holyhead Mountain hut circles*) are quite rough. Some may have been the hovels of the Anglesey copper-mine workers, but most were farms, and are often found to be set amid small fields covering in all between 2 and 20 acres

Early Christianity and the Emergence of Wales

In 410 the Emperor Honorius told the cities of Britain that they must arrange for their own defence; this was a formal recognition of political and military realities. The Empire was hard-pressed in Italy. where the sack of Rome by Alaric the Goth took place in the same year, while the barbarian sweep across Gaul two years earlier had effectively cut the normal lines of communication between Britain and the Mediterranean world. From this date there would be no more high civil and military officers appointed by the central government; the local authorities, who had always been responsible for day-to-day administration, would have also to deal with matters of high policy.

In Wales there can have been little apparent difference, at least in the earlier years. By the end of the fourth century local rulers, acting as allies of Rome, had already assumed a large measure of responsibility for local defence. At the same time a revitalization of the Atlantic seaways ensured that there was no absolute break with the classical world. It was the purpose of these contacts which changed. The Christian church, not the Imperial government, formed the new channel of communication between Gaul and the Mediterranean on one hand and the Celtic peoples of Britain and Ireland on the other.

Early Christian inscriptions

The Christian connection is reflected in the inscriptions of the fifth, sixth and seventh centuries. About a hundred of these are known in Wales. The majority record the name of the deceased, often with a simple formula such as "he lies here" ('hic iacit'). The persons commemorated are priests, who use a single name, and chieftains, who use also their patronymic. An elaborate example of the second type is to be seen on a stone found on Margam Mountain and now in *Margam Stones Museum*. The Latin inscription may be translated 'Here lies Boduoc, son of Cattegern, great grandson of Eternalis Vedomavi'. The earliest of these memorials are cut on standing pillars of stone with the Latin inscription in debased Roman capitals arranged in horizontal lines. Later examples have the lettering running vertically downwards and gradually adopt letter forms borrowed from contemporary book hands. The names recorded on the stones are British or Old Welsh, but in the south-west—the land of Dyfed—a number are inscribed in Ogham characters. Outside the south-west Ogham inscriptions extend into Glamorgan and Breconshire; there are a few in North Wales.

Ogham is a cipher consisting of long or short strokes arranged at right angles or obliquely in relation to a stem line—in Wales normally the angle or arris of the pillar stone. The cipher was an Irish

invention. Normally in Wales memorials with Oghams are bilingual with the same name in the British form in Latin letters and in the Irish form in Ogham characters. The whole process is well illustrated by another stone in *Margam Stones Museum*. It originally bore a monolingual Ogham reading 'Rolacun Maqi Illuna'. It was reused for a bilingual which reads in the Latin 'Pumpeius Carantorius'. The second Ogham, which is mutilated, can be restored as 'Pampes'.

The early Welsh Church

Tradition ascribes the conversion of the Celtic lands to missionaries, often of British origin, trained in Gaul. The 'lives' of these missionaries are generally late; in Wales the oldest surviving document is the *Life of Dewi Sant* by Rhygyfarch of St Davids, who wrote at the end of the eleventh century. Though these lives of the saints contain much that is not historical, there is no reason to reject the consistent tradition that the establishment of the Welsh church took place in the fifth and sixth centuries; the dating of the inscriptions already considered bears this out. Moreover, the location of many of the earlier inscribed stones in small family graveyards, often alongside roads, represents a survival of pre-Christian custom. The Boduoc stone (page 46), now in *Margam Stone Museum* but which stood till recently near an early settlement on Margam Mountain, and the Maen Madoc, which still stands in its original position in the uplands, beside the Roman road from the Brecon Gaer to Neath, are good examples. By the second half of the sixth century the Christian custom of churchyard burial was predominant.

The organization of the early Welsh church was based on mother churches or monasteries; the native name is 'clas', which survives as a place-name at Glasbury, near Hay, and elsewhere. The 'clas' still dominated the church in Wales at the time of the Edwardian conquest as it had throughout the early Christian period. The 'clas' was a body of men living together and following a monastic rule of life under an abbot. The community included both priests and laymen and was responsible for the pastoral care of the surrounding district. The 'clas' was often a powerful body with considerable political influence. Though many of the 'clasau' possessed substantial wealth, its members normally followed an ascetic rule of life. The individual 'clas' was often connected with a hermitage, to which the members could retire for a retreat or in old age. The solitary life in these hermitages was regarded as the highest form of religious experience and a later Welsh poet can think of no higher desire than to be buried in the 'beauteous isle of Mary' among the 'pure-souled dwellers of Enlli' (Bardsey).

St David's, Llantwit Major, Llandudoch (*St Dogmael's*), Clynnog-fawr, Bangor and *Penmon* are among the more important medieval churches which originated as 'clasau'. Of the churches and monastic buildings of the period before 1100 nothing now survives. At *Penmon* there are the *Holy Well* and a *standing cross* which is still to be seen in its original position in the Deer Park. A second cross is preserved in the church. On the neighbouring islet, Ynys Seiriol, there are also substantial remains of the associated hermitage. At Clynnogfawr, excavations revealed the foundation of a primitive oratory under the sixteenth century chapel known as 'Eglwys y Bedd' ('the church of the grave').

For the classic type of Celtic monastery or 'clas' we must go to *Tintagel* in Cornwall, where the sea-girt promontory is cut off by a large bank and ditch (the monastic 'vallum' of the texts). Inside are scattered groups of buildings, an oratory, graves, cells for the monks, buildings devoted to common use, such as the library, and finally the farm buildings, including a corn drying kiln. Air photography has recently shown that the church and cemetery of Llanafanfawr, Breconshire, occupy only a part of a great circular enclosure some 400 ft in diameter. Llanafanfawr was an important early church, probably serving the cantref of Buellt; the earthwork may well have been the 'vallum' enclosing the 'clas'. The little hermitage on Ynys Seiriol has a pear-shaped enclosure within which lie a later church and two successive groups of cells.

Church buildings of this date are practically unknown. The little oratory at Clynnogfawr can never have been the principal church of the clas. Irish analogies indicate the existence of buildings of up to 50 ft by 25 ft as early as the ninth or even the eighth century. But many churches may well have been of wood or other perishable materials, as has recently been indicated by discoveries on Burry Holms, off the Gower peninsula, and at Llandegai, near Bangor.

Holy Wells

Welsh saints are frequently associated with holy wells. Many of these are natural springs, sometimes with medicinal properties. In those cases where some structure has been erected for convenience or to prevent pollution, the surviving remains are generally of late medieval or even later date. A few may go back to an earlier period. *Ffynnon Gybi* at Llangybi (Caerns.) has two enclosed pools, into which steps descend. A cottage was added for the custodian about 1750, but the pools are known to have been resorted to for their healing properties long before that date. The masonry enclosing the pools is mortared and unlikely to be older than the twelfth century, but the use of the well can be assumed to go back to the sixth century, the age of St Cybi, after whom the parish church is named.

At *Penmon* there is a similar but simpler well-pool standing alongside a circular hut. The site lies close to the Priory Church and, like St Cybi's Well, was refurbished in the eighteenth century. The use of the well again is likely to go back to the sixth century, when St Seiriol founded the 'clas'.

On the shore of St Bride's Bay, south of St David's, are the remains of the *Chapel of St Non*, alongside which is a well, formerly enclosed in a stone roofed building with benches. The masonry of the chapel is of more than one date, the earliest part, at the base of the south wall, possibly reaching back to the seventh or eighth century, a date indicated by the stone with an incised ring cross found re-used in the later masonry.

At *St Winifred's Chapel, Holywell*, Flintshire, the architectural concept is more elaborate and entirely of the later Middle Ages, but there is no reason to doubt that the association with St Winifred goes back to a far earlier date.

Sculptured crosses

The 'clasau' or monasteries of the age of the conversion in the fifth and sixth centuries continued throughout the period to grow in wealth and influence, but the only monuments that have survived are the stone crosses which stood within the monastic enclosures or were set up elsewhere for a number of purposes. Many of these crosses are memorials placed over graves in the cemeteries, generally in those attached to the greater monasteries. Burial in these cemeteries was not confined to members of the community, but was a privilege much sought after by prominent laymen. At Llantwit Major a number of these crosses are preserved, including one set up by King Hywel of Morgannwg for his father Rhys; Hywel was ruling in the last generation of the ninth century. The fret and interlace on this cross give an indication of the date of a number of others, including such monuments as the cross which Einion set up at Margam (now in the *Margam Stones Museum*) for the soul of Gwrwared. The fret and other ornamental motives were adopted into the Welsh repertory from Saxon England. They continued in use in Wales down to the twelfth century with designs becoming less regular as direct contact with the originals was lost. Memorials of this type, often without the name of the person commemorated, are found on a number of sites including *St Dogmael's*. Among the latest are the group of headstones set up outside the south transept of the church at *Strata Florida* to commemorate Welsh princes and others; they date from after 1164, when the abbey was founded.

The graves at Strata Florida are undisturbed and illustrate the normal method of burial in this age. The body was placed in a stone box or cist made of flat slabs and a cover slab level with the surface of the ground. At the head of the grave stood a cross, in some cases apparently of wood. In the case of more important burials the cover slab is sometimes ornamented with a cross. This is a comparatively late development and examples may be noted at *St Dogmael's*. The earliest is of the ninth century and came from the cemetery of the 'clas' of Llandudoch, which was replaced in the twelfth century by the Tironian Abbey of St Dogmael's.

Crosses were also erected within the enclosure of the 'clas' to record events in the history of the community or to serve as 'foci' of devotion. Irish records provide instances of named crosses like the Cross of Columba at Kells. In Wales such traditions are lacking, but occasionally the cross itself bears a name, like the Cross of Cynfelyn (Conbelin) at Margam which still dominates the collection in *Margam Stones Museum*, though it has lost half of the height of the shaft. This is a particularly grand example, datable by its ornament to about 900 and also, exceptionally, inscribed with the name of the maker, Sodna. Such crosses must have been common in early Wales and a number are preserved in a more or less complete state in many Welsh churches, including Penally, Penmon, Diserth and Llanrhaeadr-ym-Mochnant.

These standing crosses were not confined to the monastic enclosure —they were also erected to mark church property and paths and for other purposes which can no longer be determined. One of the finest, at *Carew*, stands over 13 ft high and bears the name of Maredudd ap Edwin, King of Deheubarth from 1033 to 1035. Another—*the Pillar of Eliseg*—gives its name to the valley in Ial, where later arose the Cistercian Abbey of *Valle Crucis*, named after the cross. This dates from the ninth century and records the pedigree of Cyngen, the last king of Powys of the old line, who died in Rome in 854. The inscription, now illegible, claims that the dynasty was descended from Vortigern and Magnus Maximus, the Roman usurper, who became the Maxen Wledig of medieval romance. The connection of these two crosses with the dynasties of Deheubarth and Powys is clear, though we can no longer recover the occasion for which they were erected. The eleventh-century *Maen Achwyfan*, standing on the roadside $1\frac{1}{2}$ miles west of Whitford, is more enigmatic; it has no inscription to help unravel its original purpose. A humbler example, recording a gift to a local church, was found broken and re-used as the base of a late limekiln in the outer ward of *Ogmore Castle*.

The secular lordships

Wales in the period from 400 to 1100 formed a number of lordships, many of them grouped together under four principal dynasties. The boundaries of the principal lordships varied from time to time as did their control over the lesser chieftains.

In the north-west lay Gwynedd, covering the modern counties of Anglesey and Caernarvon, together with the greater part of Merionith. The dynasty that ruled Gwynedd claimed descent from Cunedda and his sons who came from the north, from Manau of the Gododdin, the land about the headwaters of the Forth in the modern counties of Stirling, Clackmannan and West Lothian. The Romanized character of the family is indicated by the name of Cunedda's grandfather, Padarn Beisrut (Paternus of the Red Robe), an allusion to some form of Imperial insignia. It is generally thought that the transfer of the dynasty to Wales was an act of Imperial or post-Imperial policy designed to secure the defences of the country against the Irish. Maelgwn, the great-grandson of Cunedda, whose court is traditionally located at Degannwy, died in the middle of the sixth century; his great-great-grandson, Cadfan, who died about 625, has a memorial stone in the church of Llangadwaladr, on which he is described as 'the wisest and most renowned of all kings'. The direct male line of Cunedda came to an end early in the ninth century, when Essyllt, the daughter of Cynan Tyndaethwy, married Merfyn, whose ancestors came from the Isle of Man. Merfyn's son, Rhodri Mawr (the Great) (844–77) was perhaps the most powerful of the early Welsh rulers. A vigorous policy, backed by marriage alliances, brought him dominion over the greater part of Wales, outside Glamorgan. This was only a passing achievement. The power and prosperity of Gwynedd, like that of all Wales, suffered from English aggression and Scandinavian raids and its later history down to 1100 is a story of factional strife and declining influence.

The north-east, Powys, originally comprised much of the Marches; its capital probably lay in the Roman city of Viroconium (Wroxeter, near Shrewsbury), where an early Christian inscription, in three horizontal lines and probably dating from the fifth century, has recently been found. Powys at its greatest extent reached from the Dee near Chester to the Wye in Radnorshire. Dynastic tradition, set out on the *Pillar of Eliseg* (p. 52), traced the origins of Powys to Vortigern. Powys was particularly exposed to the advance of the English. The Welsh leader in the battle of Chester (*c*. 613) was Cynan of Powys, whose son Selyf fell in the battle. The old line came to an end with the death of Cyngen in 854, after which the region split into smaller lordships. Unity was not again achieved until the time of Bleddyn ap Cynfyn in the later eleventh century.

Mathrafal, a rectangular earthwork near Meifod is traditionally associated with the rulers of Powys, but the only datable feature on site is a Norman motte. The principal monuments associated with the region are the Dykes or linear earthworks (p. 56) of which the largest bears the name of Offa, king of Mercia (757–96). This great bank and ditch runs from the estuary of the Dee to the lower Wye, with gaps marking the areas still forested in the eighth century. It was erected by the great Mercian king in order to hinder Welsh raiding, but the line chosen shows that it was a compromise in which the dominant Saxon power took some account of Welsh interests and Welsh susceptibilities. Wat's dyke, a smaller bank and ditch, and a number of short cross-ridge dykes (some of them extending far into the Welsh uplands) all form part of the frontier system, the development of which was probably spread over many generations (see pp. 56-7).

In the south-west was the kingdom of Dyfed, covering the modern county of Pembroke with much of Carmarthenshire. Both the dynasty and many of the leading men were Irish; their memorials are the Ogham inscriptions. The best known of these early rulers was Vortepor, one of the kings denounced by Gildas in the middle of the sixth century. His tombstone has the Latin inscription 'the memorial of Vortepor the Protector' together with the name alone in the Irish form Votecorigas, cut in Oghams (p. 47). It was found at Castell Dwyran and is now in the museum at Carmarthen. The office Protector, of classical origin, seems to have been used as a hereditary title. The dynasty disappears in the ninth century and Hyfaidd ap Bledri, who claimed descent from the old line through his mother, is found ruling in its stead. Hyfaidd's grand-daughter, Elen, married Hywel Dda (the Good) a grandson of Rhodri Mawr of Gwynedd. Hywel ruled over a much extended state, known as Deheubarth, which included not only the older Dyfed, but wider lands to the east and the modern county of Ceredigion, which had long been ruled by a separate dynasty claiming descent from Cunedda. During the reign of Hywel Dda old Welsh custom was codified and written down. He died about 950 and Deheubarth descended in due course to Rhys ap Teudwr, who died in 1093, in the course of the Norman invasion.

The south-east, the modern counties of Glamorgan, less Gower, and Monmouthshire, was the most Romanized part of Wales. The early history of this region is obscure. A local dynasty is recorded in the seventh century; it later split into two lines ruling respectively in Gwent (Monmouthshire) and Morgannwg (Glamorgan). None of these rulers are particularly distinguished and native rule ended in the person of Iestyn ap Gwrgant, who fell a victim to the Norman conqueror, Fitzhamon, at the end of the eleventh century.

The eleventh century is a period of unrest and confusion. It is marked by the rise to power of rulers, who could claim little or no connection with the ancient lines. Rhydderch ap Iestyn, who made himself lord of South Wales between 1023 and 1033, is one such. But more important are Llywelyn ap Seissyllt (ob. 1023) and his more powerful son, Gruffydd ap Llywelyn. The last named ruled over the greater part of Wales and carried on a long and well-fought campaign against Saxon England. He sacked Hereford in 1055 and wasted much of the Marches. His success inevitably brought an English reaction and he was betrayed and murdered in 1063. His death was quickly followed by the Norman Conquest of England and he left no successor who could organize adequate defences against the new, more formidable Norman Marcher lords.

Hill-forts

At the beginning of the period rough native pottery provides evidence of the re-occupation of some hill-forts. The Breidden on the borders of Montgomeryshire and Shropshire is an example. There, as elsewhere, few structural remains of this date have been identified and the pottery may indicate no more than temporary use as a camp of refuge. At Dinorben a re-occupation, or perhaps a continuation of the fourth century occupation, is again marked by certain types of pottery, but no structural phase.

Princely sites

A number of sites, generally defended dwellings rather than hill-forts, can be dated to this period.

Dinas Emrys, an isolated hill rising from the Gwynant valley, above Beddgelert, has a weak central enclosure, with two outworks. The slight character of the defences contrast strangely with the massive ramparts of pre-Roman hill-forts in positions of similar natural strength. Dinas Emrys was occupied in the fifth – seventh centuries and later tradition associates it with the fifth-century ruler, Ambrosius.

More usual are the smaller defended dwellings, surrounded by ramparts of stone or timber. Dinas Powis, a slight enclosure less than one acre in extent, contained two buildings of subrectangular plan, associated with imported Mediterranean pottery, glass and metal work, all attesting to a degree of wealth and sophistication in an occupation that may be dated to the fifth, sixth and seventh centuries.

A stone-built enclosure contrived within the ramparts of Garn Boduan falls into the same class; within was a circular hut. The enclosure at Garn Boduan resembles that on the summit of Garn Fadryn. This site is known to have been the residence of the sons of Owain Gwynedd at the end of the twelfth century, but the type is far older and they probably did no more than refurbish an ancestral stronghold. Another site associated with a ruler of this period is Plas Cadnant. This appears to be a small fort of the pre-Roman age, but within are rectangular dwellings; rude pottery of the type found on the Breidden has been picked up on the site. In the face of this evidence the traditional association with Cynan Tyndaethwy (ob. 816) cannot be summarily dismissed.

The evidence, slight as it is, suggests that these small defended dwelling were typical of the residence of the lords and princes of early Wales, the 'arglwyddi' who figure in the records.

Other dwellings

Of the humbler dwellings, whether of the free tribesmen or of the bond vills little can be said. The princely residences already described have both rectangular houses and hut circles. The same diversity might be expected lower down the social scale. At Pant y Saer, Anglesey, a sixth-century silver brooch suggests the continued occupation of a hut group that would otherwise have been classed as of Romano-British date. On Margam Mountain, the houses beside the original site of the *Boduoc Stone* (p. 47) are of the same type as those within the fort at Plas Cadnant, but their date has not been clearly established.

Linear earthworks

Relations between England and Wales in this period are represented on the ground by a number of linear earthworks—banks and ditches designed to protect or to prevent hostile access to the settlements of English farmers, who had penetrated into the upland valleys and reclaimed arable and pasture. The English kingdom concerned was Mercia, with its centre at Tamworth, opposite the centre of the border, at a point where the mountains project boldly towards the English midlands. The sequence and function of these earthworks were most clearly defined in a passage written by the principal worker in this field, the late Sir Cyril Fox; relevant dates have been added:

'For a hundred years (*c.* 630–*c.* 730 AD) the Mercians built "Short Dykes" as and when circumstances required in the central march, covering such mountain outliers as the Long Mynd and Wenlock Edge. Their Welsh opponents were the princes of Powys of Eliseg's dynasty. Towards the close of this phase of activity the idea of a continuous bank-and-ditch frontier was conceived, and put into practice in the geographically well defined northern sector between the upper Severn, with its tributary the Vyrnwy, and the Dee estuary. This (*ie* Wat's Dyke, built in the time of King Ethelbald, 716–757) included debatable land—Tegeingl, the east cantref of Rhos (now Flintshire) and a King of Gwynedd may have been involved. Half a century, perhaps, thereafter the final effort to define the whole west frontier of Mercia was undertaken by Offa (757–796), bringing into the picture the Kingdom of Gwent in the south. Here . . . much of the left bank of the Wye and its peninsula tip was given up, or confirmed, to Ffernfail son of Ithel or one of his sons.'

Examples of the 'short dykes' are found not only in the areas mentioned but penetrating deep into mid-Wales. Among these are the Wantyn Dyke, covering the upper Caebrita valley and Ditch Bank, blocking access to the plain of New Radnor. Place names confirm that dykes in these advanced positions represent early Mercian penetrations into the mountain zone.

Wat's Dyke was named after Wat or Wade, a Germanic folk-hero associated with Offa I of Angeln in Schleswig, a continental ancestor of Offa of Mercia. It is 38 miles long and formed a barrier designed to stop further advances by Welsh raiders, who had already penetrated into the lowlands.

Offa's Dyke is 149 miles long from Prestatyn in Flintshire to Sedbury on the Severn Sea, just east of the Wye. It consists of a bank of earth, ditched generally on the west side. The earthwork varies considerably in scale, with an average height of the bank of over 6 ft above the old surface and an average overall width of some 60 ft across bank and ditch. A fine example near Yew Tree Farm in the Parish of Discoed, Radnorshire, shows the bank 7 ft 6 in. high with an overall width of 70 ft. In country that was forested at the time of construction and where the dyke follows rivers the earthwork was not carried out. The alignment was chosen in order to control access to the lowlands and to deny to the Welsh the possibility of raiding Mercian farmlands to the east; tactically it is set out in order to give as wide a view westwards as possible. Offa's Dyke (Clawdd Offa) represents an agreed frontier with the Welsh, though the design and execution were purely English. Today, after more than 1000 years, it remains with no more than minor modifications the boundary line of Cymru, and is followed along much of its length by the long-distance footpath formally opened by Lord Hunt in 1971.

The Middle Ages

by GLANMOR WILLIAMS, MA, D Litt., FR Hist. Soc.

Historical survey

THE early Welsh had an unhappy propensity for quarrelling violently among themselves. As Gerald of Wales, that astute commentator on their national characteristics, observed: 'From this cause continual fratricides take place . . . and whence arise murders, conflagrations and almost a total destruction of the country.' This was never more true of any period than of the century or so between 949 and 1066, when no fewer than 35 Welsh rulers are known to have met a violent death, four more were blinded, and another four imprisoned. Any measure of unity brought about by a powerful ruler like Hywel Dda ('the Good') who ruled c. 920–950, or Gruffudd ap Llywelyn (1039–63) was too fragile to outlive the reign in which it was achieved. The effects of Welsh feuds, aggravated by Anglo-Saxon interventions and Viking raids, kept the country politically feeble and divided. Wales's independence was maintained precariously alive only by its difficult terrain and by the relative ineffectuality of its neighbour, the Old English kingdom, which was strong enough to threaten but too weak to extinguish Welsh autonomy. Even so, the remarkably resolute campaign successfully mounted by Harold, son of Godwin, in 1063 pointed clearly to the potential danger of the military subjugation of Wales by the Old English kingdom.

The danger that had been latent before 1066 became actual once the Norman kingdom was capable of exploiting the potential of the Old English polity to the point of making itself the most powerful state in western Europe. It was unlikely to tolerate unmoved the existence along its western flank of a group of turbulent independent Welsh kinglets. Furthermore, the Conqueror and his companions, schooled by the stern necessities of life in their Norman duchy, were a closely-knit military élite, an aristocracy organized for war. They numbered in their ranks some of the most hardened and efficient exponents of frontier defence to be found anywhere in Europe. This fact of Norman life Wales soon learnt to its cost. As early as 1067 William I planted at Hereford one of his ablest lieutenants, William Fitzosbern. Fitzosbern, having rapidly established himself in the border castles of Wigmore, Clifford and Ewyas Harold, soon overran the Welsh-speaking area of Herefordshire known as Archenfield. He then penetrated into Wales proper and, between 1067 and 1071, had built a number of forts along the line of the Dore-Monnow-Wye, from Clifford in the north through Monmouth to Chepstow in the south. Before his death in 1071 he had pressed deeper into Wales to seize a great part of the country westward to the Usk. His exploits had already set the pattern for the future Norman conquest of much of southern and eastern Wales: piecemeal initiative by an ambitious and vigorous frontier lord; rapid military penetration followed by quick consolidation with castles at strategic points; and seizure of the political and legal rights of Welsh rulers as well as their land in order to create new and virtually independent Norman lordships.

In Mid and North Wales the keys to Norman expansion were the palatine earldoms of Shrewsbury and Chester where, in 1071, Roger of Montgomery and Hugh of Avranches were respectively installed. Earl Roger and his brood of warlike sons, thrusting up the valley of the Severn, established a main base for the conquest of Mid-Wales at Montgomery, to which they gave their name. By 1086 they were already perched in the hilly wilds of the Plynlimmon region ready to descend into south-west Wales as soon as the opportunity offered. Further north, Earl Hugh of Chester entrusted the task of breaking into North Wales to his energetic kinsman and lieutenant, Robert of Rhuddlan, so called after the castle he had built by 1073 on the bank of the River Clwyd, whose marshy unreclaimed estuary at this time formed a major natural barrier into the heart of North Wales. Rhuddlan, as the lowest fording-place on the river, was to prove a key point in the six-century-long struggle (*c.* 700–1300) between Welsh and English along this northern border. Another hardly less crucial point was Degannwy on the Conwy estuary where, by 1075, Robert of Rhuddlan had set up a castle as his forward base. Robert's dramatic successes had within a few years led William I to recognize him as his lieutenant of all North Wales (potential rather than actual), holding it directly of the Crown. Following Robert's death in 1088, Earl Hugh himself took up the task of conquest. He pushed on deep into the heart of Gwynedd building a castle at Aberlleiniog in Anglesey and another at *Caernarvon*, a primitive fore-runner of the huge Edwardian fortress now standing there.

Meantime, down in south-west Wales, a native Welsh ruler, Rhys ap Tewdwr, was recognized by William I as a vassal, a kind of Welsh southern counterpart to Robert of Rhuddlan. This shrewd stroke by the Welshman was instrumental in keeping the Normans at arm's length for some years. But Rhys's death in 1093 shattered the dam that had hitherto stemmed the tide of Norman encroachment into the south and west. From all sides now, the Normans poured through in such a way as to suggest a pre-concerted plan, though it may in fact represent no more than the unleashing of a number of eager individual ventures. The Montgomery family, led by Roger's son, Arnulf, swept swiftly through Ceredigion as far south as Pembroke. Near Carmarthen William Fitzbaldwin, sheriff of Devon, was actively planting a lordship on the king's behalf. The de Braose family moved into Radnor, and Bernard of Neufmarché completed his conquest of Brycheiniog (Brecknock). Most significant and longest-lasting in its effects was the rapid overrunning of Morgannwg (Glamorgan) by Robert Fitzhamon from his base in Gloucester. The net effect of all these incursions by the middle of William II's reign was to make it appear likely that the whole of Wales would fall easily into Norman hands.

Appearances proved deceptive, however. If Wales was a country of hill, moor and mountain not easily united, it was, by the same token, a land not lightly conquered. The speed and suddenness of this first phase of conquest acted like shock-therapy on the Welsh. They had not at first realized how dangerous an adversary the Norman was likely to be, and his initial victory over the hated Saxon had not been entirely unwelcome to them. They had even supposed they could with impunity invite him in as an ally in their own endless feuds and rivalries. Now, however, fully aroused to the swiftness and brutality of the Norman threat, they countered with furious uprisings aimed at ejecting the invaders. Between 1094 and 1098 there were on-slaughts against the Normans in most parts of Wales. Led mainly by the ruling families of Powys and Gwynedd they achieved consider-able success, particularly in the remoter and more rugged areas of the north and west. But when the waves of revolt finally subsided, the strongest rocks of Norman power in the south and east re-appeared largely intact. The intruders were still in undismayed possession of all their key bases and could resume heavy pressure on the Welsh. Behind his frontier lords stood the formidable Henry I (1100–35), seen by the Welsh chronicler as 'the man with whom none may strive, save God Himself, who hath given him the dominion'. This 'divinely-ordained' power was felt by much of Wales. In Pem-broke, Carmarthen (thereafter always a royal lordship), Cardigan, Kidwelly, and Gower, Henry's friends and vassals, including a large colony of Flemings in south Pembrokeshire, were firmly installed. The Welsh rulers of Deheubarth and Powys were particularly con-scious of his iron hand pressing tightly upon them.

By the first quarter of the twelfth century, indeed, all the essentials of the pattern and rhythm of the relationships between the Welsh and the Normans for the next 150 years were already in existence. Between the kingdom of England and the independent Welsh lands of the north and west lay the Norman lordships of the March (from French 'marche'—frontier) carved out by the restless initiative of a couple of generations of tough and venturesome Norman lords. The March swung in a rough arc south from Chester to Chepstow and thence west to Pembroke. At some points, between Hereford and Llandovery, it widened to as much as 50 miles across, and at others, between Cardiff and the northern limits of Brecon lordship, it was some 50 miles deep. Most of it had been won by the sword. Small groups of armoured Norman knights and men-at-arms, often taking advantage of local vendettas among the Welsh, had pushed determinedly in to seize the latter's territory. Once the intruders had gained a foothold, almost their first reaction had been to throw up castles, usually of motte-and-bailey construction with earthworks and wooden defences (see below, pp. 72-3). Primitive as these castles were by later standards they offered their occupants strongpoints from which they were not easily dislodged. The castles were invaluable in subduing and holding what had already been won and as a springboard for further expansion. Even in those rare instances when a Norman lord took possession by means other than conquest as, for instance, when Henry de Newburgh, Earl of Warwick, obtained his lordship of Gower from Henry I *c.* 1105 seemingly without having to fight for it, castles were quickly constructed.

As a means for undermining Welsh resistance the new Norman lords seized not only the lands of Welsh rulers but also the sovereign rights that went with them. These rights had in pre-Norman Wales been based on the Welsh territorial division known as the commote (Welsh 'cwmwd'), which was the unit of political, judicial and administrative authority. It now became the unit of incursion and conquest, when the old commote was in many instances turned into the new lordship. Within its boundaries the lord ruled like a little king, enjoying such prerogatives as holding his own courts with rights of life and death, levying taxes, minting coins, creating boroughs and even making war. Each lordship had its own 'caput' or capital, where its chief castle was built. This served not merely as a stronghold and barracks but also as a home for the lord and his family and servants, a financial and administrative headquarters, a prison and a court of justice. To provide for the needs of such a castle it was usually necessary to create a borough. Its burgesses, at first drawn strictly from a non-Welsh population, were given a charter of privileges normally embodying exclusive trading rights and limited rights of justice and self-government. In this, as in other respects, William Fitzosbern was the pioneer. He conferred upon Hereford a charter based on that of his borough of Breteuil in Normandy; and this, in turn, served as a model for most of the boroughs of the March. Many of the oldest towns of South Wales—Chepstow, Abergavenny, Monmouth, Cardiff, Brecon, Neath, Swansea, Kidwelly, Haverfordwest, and Pembroke, to name but a few—owe their origin to such a development. Similar steps had been taken in parts of North Wales. As early as 1086 Domesday Book recorded that Rhuddlan had its borough rights, based on those of Hereford, and that it also boasted a mint, some of whose silver coins still survive in national collections.

Each Marcher lordship had its own autonomous organization; but the general pattern in each was very similar. Many lordships were divided into two parts; the Englishry and the Welshry. The former usually covered the more favoured low-lying areas below the 600 ft or even the 400 ft contour. It was usually divided up into knight's fees to be held by the lord's vassals on condition of loyal service. These vassals, in turn, constructed lesser castles or fortified houses for their own security. In the Englishry, manorial farming, with its customary features of open fields and unfree labour service, was often introduced. The Englishry was also separately administered with its own officials and courts of justice in which an amalgam of Anglo-Norman law and custom normally prevailed. By contrast, in the upland areas lay the Welshry. Here the old Welsh laws and customs still continued, and so, too, did traditional Welsh agricultural and pastoral practices. The inhabitants came very largely under the authority of their own native ruling families and owed only a shadowy allegiance to the Norman overlord. Passionately devoted still to their own language, culture and *mores*, they lived with their Norman overlords on terms not far short of an armed neutrality which not infrequently broke out into open hostility and insurrection.

Another instrument for undermining Welsh resistance, at first sight improbable enough for the purpose but one which the Normans used with marked effect, was the Church. The piety of the Norman ruling classes as evinced in their native duchy before 1066 was real enough of its kind, but carried within it a broad streak of characteristically down-to-earth practicality. It was expressed in two highly typical ways. The first took the form of a rough conventional devotion which aimed at vicariously appeasing the Deity for many a bloody deed and carnal transgression by means of lavish endowments to a number of abbeys in Normandy which had come under the influence of Cluny or some other reform movement. The second was the creation of a close-knit body of aristocrat-bishops intimately linked with and dependent upon the duke and his leading barons. Both methods were successfully transported across the Channel to England and Wales.

Having arrived in Wales, the Normans had neither understanding of the institutions of the Celtic Church they found there, nor any sympathy with them. They consequently wasted no time in applying to the Church those familiar methods which had worked so well in Normandy. In the process they broke up many of the old 'clasau' of Wales and, promptly laying hands on the patrimony of these ancient institutions, they transferred it to favoured abbeys in France or England. The trendsetter here again was Fitzosbern. It was he who created at Chepstow a daughter priory to the abbey at Cormeilles which he himself had founded. Other Norman lords quickly followed suit. Goldcliff Priory was affiliated to the Norman abbey of Bec. Abergavenny to St Vincent of Le Mans, Monmouth to St Florent of Saumur, Llangenydd to St Taurin of Evreux, and Pembroke to St Martin at Séez. Brecon Priory, on the other hand, was a daughter of Battle, *Kidwelly* of Sherborne, and *Ewenny* of St Peter's, Gloucester, an abbey which, together with Tewkesbury, was richly and freely endowed in Glamorgan. In addition to so handsomely patronizing the Benedictine Order the Normans were also responsible for introducing three of the new reformed monastic Orders into Wales —those associated with Tiron, Savigny and Cîteaux. The Tironian Order founded the abbey of *St Dogmael's* far away in Pembrokeshire some time before 1120. The Savignacs gained a foothold at *Neath* in South Wales in 1130 and at *Basingwerk* in the north in the same year. Even the Cistercians, the Order most intimately and readily associated with the life of Wales, first came to the country under the Norman aegis when they were established at *Tintern* in 1131 and Margam in 1147. It was the Normans, also, who encouraged the founding of communities of Augustinian canons in South Wales—at *Llanthony* in 1103, and later at Carmarthen (before 1143) and Haverfordwest (before 1200). But while individual lords were free to dispense their bounty to abbeys as they saw fit, control of the episcopate brought weightier forces into play. This was a sphere in which the King and the Archbishop of Canterbury were to have the leading voice. In 1107 Henry I and Anselm obliged the new Bishop of Llandaff to make the first profession of obedience by a Welsh bishop to the see of Canterbury. By the middle of the twelfth century bishops of all four Welsh dioceses had been induced to do the same. The degree of subordination to which bishops were subjected varied widely. Though all the bishops were obliged to recognize the spiritual authority of Canterbury, the measure of freedom from lay control they enjoyed was markedly different. The Bishop of St David's was a Marcher lord in his own right; but the Bishop of Llandaff came very much under the thumb of the lord of Glamorgan, while the Bishop of Bangor was hardly better than the domestic chaplain of the prince of Gwynedd. However, in all the Welsh dioceses there now took place a thorough reorganization. For the first time the dioceses became territorially defined, and within the new diocesan boundaries other new territorial units—archdeaconries, rural deaneries and parishes—were instituted. They provided the machinery for the introduction of the stricter canons of Roman discipline.

Admirably though these changes in the Church served the turn of the Normans, it would be wrong to think of them simply as expedients for political subjugation. The conquest had far-reaching consequences for good. The isolation of the pre-Conquest church in Wales carried with it the peril of stagnation as the price of autonomy. Breaking down this isolation, the Normans threw the Church open to fresh and invigorating streams of reform flowing strongly from that fountainhead of early medieval religious inspiration, the reformed papacy.

So, over large areas of the territorial, political and ecclesiastical life of Wales, King and baronage had combined to impose their will. Yet the relationship between suzerain and vassals was an ambivalent one. Some of these lords held extensive territories on both sides of the Channel and enjoyed such far-reaching prerogatives as lords of the March as to make them almost rival potentates to the King. Dangers from them emerged at an early stage; the son of William Fitzosbern was deprived of his lands for sedition in 1075, and the Montgomery family were in deep disgrace in 1102. But, in the last resort, King and lords had each too much need of the other to abandon one another for long. The lords, without the backing of royal armies, would often have been in desperate straits from Welsh insurrections; and the king, for his part, could not risk a permanently unsettled or weakened western frontier.

Meantime, both king and Marcher lords had to adjust their relationships with the Welsh rulers of the north and west. The latter, though frequently still bitterly divided among themselves, were always watchful of an opportunity to press their advantage against the Norman invaders. England's difficulty could be their opportunity. Thus these Welsh rulers could turn to good account such sources of English weakness as the anarchy of Stephen's reign (1135–54), or the conflict between Henry II and Becket (1162–70), or Richard I's preoccupation with the Crusades (1189–99). Nevertheless, during the long reign of Henry II (1154–89) some kind of unstable equilibrium was coming into being. The rulers of Wales recognized the King as overlord; in return they were conceded virtual autonomy within their own lands. This was effectively exploited by the ablest among them: Owain Gwynedd (1137–70) and the Lord Rhys of Deheubarth (c. 1155–97). Not the least of their achievements was that they learnt many lessons from their enemies. They had always been considerable masters of guerrilla warfare. Now they came to appreciate the importance of having castles of their own and of learning the tactics needed to reduce their enemies' strongholds. They also learned to win and use the support of the Church. Their scope for initiative in the control of the bishops and the hierarchy was limited; but in the patronage of religious Orders they could and did achieve much more success. The Benedictines they always rejected because they were too closely associated with the Normans. However, they were willing to encourage the Order of Augustinian canons to take over the former Celtic houses of *Penmon*, Bardsey and Beddgelert. The Cistercians found even more favour in Welsh eyes (see p. 92). In return, the White Monks became more closely associated than any other clerics with the political aspirations of the princes and with the literary and patriotic associations of Wales.

The full scope of this Welsh renaissance was not achieved until the thirteenth century. Although in Deheubarth and Powys by this time the ruling families were reduced to fragmented groups of ineffectual rivals, Gwynedd was the scene of a remarkable essay in state-building. This was the achievement of its two most gifted rulers: Llywelyn ab Iorwerth ('the Great', 1194–1240) and his grandson, Llywelyn ap Gruffudd ('the Last', 1247–82). Each contrived to exploit to his own benefit those conflicts in which the English Crown from time to time found itself embroiled with France, or the Church, or a disaffected baronage. Both princes successfully applied to Welsh conditions the statecraft and military science of the thirteenth century. They tried to adapt and modernize Welsh institutions to strengthen the authority of the prince of Gwynedd. His vague claim to supremacy over other Welsh rulers was turned into a successful assertion of his feudal overlordship. Customary Welsh law was modified to restrict the influence of the kindred and to give keener edge to the jurisdiction of the prince. The growing population was encouraged to adopt a more closely-defined and intensive pattern of agricultural settlement; early native boroughs were established at places like Pwllheli and Caernarvon, and trade was fostered. Such expedients made in turn for more effective control and taxation to finance ambitious political policies and the military backing needed for them. A number of fairly highly-developed castles capable of withstanding improved methods of siege warfare, such as those at *Castell y Bere*, *Dolbadarn* and *Dolforwyn*, were constructed. Favoured followers were given lands on conditions of military tenure, and from among them came some of the prince's most trusted lieutenants. Able servants were also drawn from among the religious Orders favourable to the princes and generously supported by them, chief among them the already-established Cistercians and the new Orders of friars, who spread widely in thirteenth-century Wales with warm princely encouragement. The high-water mark of these state-building policies was reached at the Treaty of Montgomery of 1267. Concluded between Henry III and Llywelyn ap Gruffudd, it accorded Llywelyn the title of Prince of Wales and recognized him as overlord of a large part of the country. This was as near to a position of legal independence as he could hope to come.

Llywelyn's newly-won authority lasted no longer than ten years. In acquiring it he had awakened the suspicion of the King of England, the alarm of Marcher lords, and the resentment of many of his own countrymen. His position was, at best, one that needed careful nursing. Yet after the accession of Edward I in 1272, Llywelyn seemed almost to go out of his way to court the King's anger. For four years he seemed unable or unwilling to recognize how powerful was this most formidable of medieval English kings. He refused the homage and the money payments owing under the treaty and arranged to marry the daughter of Edward's former arch-enemy, Simon de Montfort. The considerations which may have impelled the Welsh prince to so rash a course—over-confidence, mis-reading the political omens, under-estimating his enemies' strength—remain uncertain. What is not open to question is the grave retribution his miscalculation provoked. By 1276 Edward I, publicly exasperated beyond endurance but secretly not wholly displeased perhaps, had resolved to settle his account with the recalcitrant Welsh prince. Edward, a warrior-king who was his own commander-in-chief, using Chester, Montgomery and Carmarthen as bases, during the winter of 1276–77 exerted pressure on Llywelyn's outlying possessions so as to pen him in Gwynedd. By midsummer 1277 he was ready to send a fleet to Anglesey to cut the Welsh off from their corn supply, while his main army moved along the narrow coastal strip. Flint and Rhuddlan marked the stages in the advance to Degannwy at the mouth of the Conwy. Meantime his army in South Wales was pressing up the Towy Valley into Cardigan. Llywelyn, confronted with vastly superior odds, had no choice but to negotiate from a position of weakness. Humiliation predictably followed; the Treaty of Aberconway (1277) stripped him of his feudal overlordship and most of his territory outside Gwynedd, though it left him with the now almost empty title of Prince of Wales.

The events of 1276–77 seem to have been for Llywelyn a traumatic experience which destroyed all his earlier illusions. He was now painfully anxious to fulfil all his commitments to Edward. Nor did Edward give him much choice. From the outset in 1276 the King seems to have been set on constructing a series of powerful castles at *Flint*, *Rhuddlan*, Aberystwyth and Builth which would confine the lion of Gwynedd within his ancestral mountain lair. Edward now firmly installed his own men at these new castles as well as in older-established bases like Degannwy, Carmarthen, Cardigan and *Carreg Cennen*. These English officials ruled the country with a mailed fist and provoked a deal of discontent among the Welsh. Edward also

Dolbadarn Castle

Castell y Bere

comforted Llywelyn's Welsh enemies and kept him waiting for legal redress of his complaints. Yet Llywelyn himself refused to be provoked. It was his brother Dafydd, Edward's ally in 1277 ironically enough, who, in March 1282, raised the flag of Welsh revolt. But once it had been hoisted, all Llywelyn's instincts and experience drove him inexorably into joining the insurrection. This time it was a fight to the finish and as such was more bitter and protracted than had been the campaign of 1276–77. Edward's strategy was much the same as it had been earlier: all-round pressure in West Wales and the Marches, and in the north a sea-borne occupation of Anglesey to coincide with coastal advance to the Conwy.

In November 1282 a premature crossing from Anglesey to the mainland brought a serious disaster for the English army; but Edward remained undeterred. Even before the news reached him in the next month of Llywelyn's death in mysterious circumstances near Builth in December 1282, Edward had determined to fight a winter campaign whatever the difficulties. His tenacity was rewarded. In January 1283 he captured *Dolwyddelan Castle*, focal point of Snowdonia's communications, and so opened the road to all parts of Gwynedd. Two other major Welsh strongpoints, *Dolbadarn* and *Castell y Bere*, were overcome, and Prince Dafydd was reduced to skulking the countryside like a hunted animal. By the summer he, too, was captured and executed. The odds had been too great; Gwynedd had been militarily crushed and its princes killed. With them died the independence of Wales.

Edward had won more complete success over the Welsh in the field of battle than any previous English ruler had done, but he was too much the realist not to appreciate that Welsh princes had been beaten before, only to reappear or be replaced disconcertingly quickly. This time he intended that the defeat should be final. No Welsh successor to Llywelyn, direct or indirect, would be recognized in Gwynedd; this heartland of Welsh political independence and aspiration would be brought under direct royal rule. The transference of jurisdiction from Welsh to English royalty was symbolized within a few years (1301) by conferring the title and status of Prince of Wales upon the King's eldest son, a practice which has since been traditional in the British royal family. Even before that, from 1284 onwards, Edward had embarked upon a thorough-going process of subjugating newly-conquered north-west Wales; militarily, administratively, and legally. Militarily, royal strategy was based on the construction of a series of magnificent castles—notably at *Caernarvon, Conwy, Beaumaris* and *Harlech* (see pp. 81–2). The logistics of supply the castle garrisons were ensured by creating for each castle its own adjacent borough, planted with officials, traders and craftsmen. To encourage English and foreign burgesses to come there Edward offered them a guarantee against loss and banned trade in the major commodities of Wales (oxen, cows, horses and other wares) from all places except the boroughs. As a further attraction the King in some instances built fine town walls to protect his burgesses. These walls, still so memorably part of the townscape at *Conwy* and *Caernarvon*, were themselves an extension of the castle's defences. They illustrate the interlocking roles of castle and borough in the task of safeguarding security, commerce and conquest. Yet at Caernarvon, outside the walls, Edward allowed the old Welsh township to continue side by side with his new borough, a symbol perhaps of his hope that the conquered Welsh population might also come to recognize the value of his boroughs as convenient markets and ports.

The castles and boroughs also had an administrative and legal function. They were to be the centres of the new administration by which Edward intended to extend into North Wales English methods which had for a long time proved their worth to the Crown in its government of the royal lordships of Carmarthen and Cardigan in the south. Gwynedd was now divided into the three new shires of Anglesey, Caernarvon and Merioneth, and these were further subdivided into hundreds based on the former commotes. In the northeast the new county of Flint was carved out and attached to the county palatine of Chester. Within these shires Edward established the usual shire officers of sheriff and coroner, but at the lower levels of the commote he kept the customary Welsh officers known as the 'rhingyll' and 'rhaglaw'. The shires were grouped together for the purposes of finance and justice, with an exchequer and chancery at Caernarvon, and two similar institutions for the south-west at Carmarthen. Legally, Edward introduced many of the provisions of English criminal law and also a number of English judicial procedures.

The King's settlement of Wales was characteristically statesmanlike and practical. Nor was it by any means wholly unacceptable to the Welsh. Some of them had been becoming restive under the increasing weight of Prince Llywelyn's authority and were able to accept without much embarrassment the exchange of an English master for a Welsh one. Some leading Welsh families were prepared to cooperate with the English authorities by holding office at the level of the commote. A favoured few even aspired to higher things like the office of sheriff of a county or constable of a castle. Many other Welshmen looked for fame, fortune and adventure by fighting in the English armies in their many battles against the Scots and the French. The skill and ferocity of Welsh archers were much in demand. They fought with distinction in battles like Falkirk (1298), or later with the Black Prince at Creçy (1346) and Poitiers (1356). Meanwhile, in Wales itself, English law and customs of land-holding were slowly becoming more widely adopted. Together with the spread of trade and a money economy they were gradually breaking down the subsistence pastoral economy and the kindred institutions of Wales. Yet Edward wisely made no attempt to proscribe the Welsh language or to suppress the literary culture of Wales, which now moved into its golden era. In these respects it might have appeared as if a slow peaceful assimilation of Wales into the English state was unhurriedly maturing.

There were, however, other darker aspects of the Welsh scene. Edward's conquest still left Wales divided between the royal lands of the Principality and the feudal lordships of the March, with the latter remaining as autonomous, fragmented and turbulent as before. If the Welsh population of both areas were to become reconciled to the loss of their independence much would depend on the spirit in which the régime in both Principality and March was administered. All too often, unfortunately, the attitude of officialdom in both areas was self-interested and oppressive. Moreover, the fourteenth and fifteenth centuries were almost bound to be a difficult and unsettled period anyway. This was an age of war, heavy taxation, plague, depopulation and depression, when there was always an incipient risk of rebellion. All the more so among a people only very partially willing to accept the idea of conquest and still cherishing prophecies, assiduously kept evergreen by the bards, of an ultimate victory for the Welsh nation, led by a prince of destiny, over the alien usurpers. Within ten years of Edward's conquest there had been serious rebellions led by Rhys ap Maredudd (1287) and Madog ap Llywelyn (1294). The surprising thing perhaps is that there was not more trouble in Wales; especially when England was heavily involved in war with France and Scotland, both of which from time to time recognized the possibility of exploiting for their own advantage Welsh hostility to the English. Such dangers were thrown into sharp relief in 1370–72. At this time Owain Lawgoch ('of the Red Hand'), a descendant of the princes of Gwynedd who had taken service in the armies of the King of France, threatened to return to Wales to claim his inheritance with French help. Much more formidable was the rebellion (1400–15) of Owain Glyndŵr. Intensely imbued with a consciousness of being the deliverer foretold by the prophecies, he appealed to Scotland, Ireland and France for help in setting up an independent Welsh state. For a time he achieved remarkable success; he virtually extinguished English authority over a large part of Wales, captured great castles like *Harlech* and Aberystwyth and

closely besieged others, like *Caernarvon*. But his rebellion ended in
failure and bequeathed a disastrous aftermath of physical destruction, economic malaise and sapped morale. Wales had far from
recovered from these ills when the civil wars broke out between the
rival factions of Lancaster and York. Both sides drew a good deal
of military strength from the disturbed and warlike areas of Wales
and the March. In the course of these internecine struggles some
of the greater castles of Wales were strongpoints of considerable
strategic importance and changed hands more than once.

In 1485, after a generation or more of inconclusive faction, feud and
civil war, a long-suffering population might have been forgiven for
seeing in the victory of Henry VII at Bosworth only the fleeting
success of yet another transient and short-lived occupant of the
English throne. As it turned out, however, his accession marked the
end of the wars and the inauguration of the most successful ruling
house in British history. The dynasty which Henry Tudor founded
was one for which the Welsh had a particular place in their affec-
tions. In the accession of Henry VII, scion of an Anglesey stock
claiming descent from the old Welsh ruling families and himself born
in Pembroke Castle, his Welsh compatriots saw the triumphant
vindication of all the ancient prophecies which had foretold the
eventual restoration to a member of the ancient royal house of Wales
a place of rightful rule over the whole island of Britain. As the
prophesied 'man of destiny', Henry drew to himself the hearts of
Welshmen 'as lodestone doth the iron', in the words of George
Owen, the most famous of Welsh antiquaries of the Tudor period.
This mystique of Welsh loyalty and affection was transmitted from
Henry to his descendants. Nor did this more co-operative Welsh
attitude towards the Crown of England go wholly unrequited. Henry
VII offered something of a 'new deal' to some of his Welsh subjects
by entrusting leading figures among them with some of the highest
offices in Wales and encouraging others to migrate to England in
search of wealth and position.

His son Henry VIII went further. By the parliamentary 'Acts of
Union' of 1536 and 1542–43 he merged the whole of Wales into
England. For the first time he gave Wales a uniform system of law,
justice and administration based on existing institutions in England.
The March was at last finally swept away, and the whole of Wales
was shired and given all the paraphernalia and personnel of shire
administration, including assize courts and quarter sessions, parliamentary representatives, sheriffs and justices of the peace. The Welsh
language was not proscribed but was relegated to an inferior position, and English was made the language of law, administration and
record. The strong rule of the Tudors exercised through the Privy

Council, Council of the Marches and the organs of local government brought a greater measure of peace, order and stability. There was still a fair amount of sporadic violence and disorder but nothing to compare with the anarchy and insecurity of the fifteenth century. Parallel with the improved state of public security had gone the growth of population and the economic recovery common to many parts of western Europe. Estates were expanded and consolidated, agricultural methods were improved, industrial resources began to be tentatively exploited, and commerce revived. These stabler and more prosperous conditions were reflected in the decay of medieval castles. They had outlived their purpose and many were allowed to fall into ruin. Others, like *Raglan*, *Oxwich* or Laugharne, were remodelled and turned into more peaceful and comfortable country houses, not unlike the new town and country mansions now being built for a quieter, wealthier and more law-abiding age. The day of the castles was over except for a short interlude during the civil wars of the seventeenth century (1642–46 and 1648–50) when they were once again put to warlike uses. For a few brief storm-laden years castles like *Raglan*, *Montgomery* and Pembroke once more became vital strongholds bitterly fought over.

The decline of the castles was slower and less dramatic than the end of another highly characteristic medieval institution, the monastery. Monasteries in England and Wales were swept away as the result of Henry VIII's repudiation of papal authority in 1534. When once Henry and his chief adviser, Thomas Cromwell, had made the king Supreme Head of the English Church, almost their very next step was to transfer a large part of its property to the royal possession. Following a survey in 1535 of the material endowments and spiritual condition of the religious houses, an act of 1536 dissolved all of them with a clear annual income of less than £200. All the Welsh monasteries except three disappeared under this Act. For those which survived—Whitland, *Neath* and *Strata Florida*—the respite was short-lived; they, too, had gone by 1539. In Wales the end of the medieval phase of government and law coincided remarkably closely with the end of the Middle Ages in religion.

Castles

Motte-and-bailey castles

CASTLES are the characteristic product of the feudal Europe that emerged in the ninth and tenth centuries AD amid the disintegration of the empire founded by Charlemagne in 800. Scholars are now divided in their views whether or not there were castles of some kind in Britain before the Norman Conquest, but it is quite certain that if the Normans did not actually introduce the castle into England

and subsequently into Wales they made much more effective use of it than anyone else had previously done and turned it into the indispensable instrument of their conquest and consolidation. Some of the earliest and strongest of these castles were placed at the main centres of Norman power along the border with Wales: Chester, Shrewsbury, Hereford, Gloucester and Bristol. From these bases Norman magnates pressed forward into Wales, consolidating their position with castles, which were not massive and elaborate stone buildings but earth-and-timber structures known as motte-and-bailey castles. These consisted of two parts. The first, the motte, was the stronghold and consisted of a mound usually some 20 to 30 ft in height (either a natural hillock scarped and shaped, or an artificially constructed mound of heaped earth) surmounted by wooden buildings within a palisade and defended all round by a moat, wet or dry, with its counterscarp. At Cardiff the original motte, now surmounted by a stone tower, can still be clearly seen, while at Rhuddlan the Norman motte, now known as '*The Twthill*', rises plainly visible a short distance to the south-east of the Edwardian castle. Adjoining the motte were one or more baileys. The bailey was an oval or right-angled enclosure with one gateway at the furthest point away from the motte. It, too, was defended by ditch and rampart and by a stockade which ran up the side of the motte to join the palisade at the top. Access from bailey to motte was gained only by means of a sloping bridge across the ditch between the two. The whole area might encompass about 1½ acres, increasing in some instances to a maximum of about 3 acres. This is the kind of castle which can be seen so graphically illustrated in the Bayeux Tapestry, where there are scenes of men at work constructing such fortifications.

In addition to the motte-and-bailey castle proper there is a variation of this type of defence-work usually described as a ring-motte. Where this occurs the circular area on which the wooden keep was built was not raised above the general level of its surroundings but was protected by steep banks of earth dug from the surrounding ditch.

Some motte-and-bailey castles were later rebuilt in stone, sometimes preserving the outlines of their motte-and-bailey origins. At *Cilgerran* the inner ward of the castle occupies the site of the motte and the outer ward that of the bailey. At *Skenfrith*, where the motte can still be seen, we know that as late as 1187–88 money was still being spent on the timber defences which surrounded it. *Tretower* preserves the remains of a motte that had to be revetted with a stone wall at an early date because of the softness of the soil from which it was made. The encircling ditch of the ring-motte at *Llawhaden* can still be seen, although the bank had subsequently been levelled and covered with later buildings.

Dolwyddelan Castle

Chepstow Castle

Early stone castles

The earliest Norman stone building known in Wales was part of *Chepstow Castle* where, before 1071, William Fitzosbern erected an oblong tower of two storeys made of stone and also raised part of a stone curtain wall. This was exceptional, but from the twelfth century onwards more and more stonework began to appear. This did not, of course, mean that timber structures were replaced wholesale in a very short space. At *Rhuddlan* even in 1241–42 part at least of the defences was still made of wood, as they may have been at *Raglan* as late as 1400. The process of replacement in stone was gradual, continuous and piecemeal, and since stone buildings called for greater skill and much more money than those of earth and timber only a minority of motte-and-bailey castles were so rebuilt and many of the lesser examples were abandoned. The first stone or partly-stone castles of the second half of the twelfth century and the early part of the thirteenth were thus the lineal descendants of the motte-and-bailey castles and 'grew' out of them. The process of strengthening in stone began, understandably, with what had formerly been the motte, replacing it usually by a powerful stone keep with the entrance at the first-floor level, which generally contained the lord's chief residence, although many of the smaller examples hardly seem to have been large enough to have served this purpose. The ruins of a number of keeps dating from the twelfth century can be seen in Wales. *Ogmore* has a rectangular keep of rather rough construction, though part of it is skilfully dressed with ashlar, going back to the early part of the twelfth century, possibly indeed to the period of its founder, William de Londres (died *c*. 1126). Two neighbouring castles, *Coity* and *Newcastle* (Bridgend, Glam.) have each a square keep and a curtain wall of late twelfth-century date. Even more striking, perhaps, is the thirteenth-century rectangular keep at *Dolwyddelan*, which was obviously once surrounded by a courtyard enclosed by a timber stockade, later rebuilt in stone. The particular interest of Dolwyddelan is that it was built by one of the Welsh princes, thus showing how the latter had learnt from their enemies something of the art of military architecture.

Square and rectangular keeps, because of their weight, were not usually built on the motte itself but on ground level near it. A more common form of refortifying the motte in stone, therefore, was the shell keep consisting of a circular or polygonal wall built round the top of the motte in place of the earlier palisade. Along with the building of a shell keep of this sort went very often the replacement of the palisade of the bailey by a stone wall which was carried up two sides of the motte to join the keep. An unusually good example of this technique can still be seen at Cardiff and another at *Tretower*

Castle in Breconshire. A modified expedient of the same kind was adopted at Carmarthen, where the stone wall of the shell keep was built at the base of the motte and carried up as a revetment wall to the whole mound.

The thirteenth century brought further improvements in fortification. The twelfth-century square and rectangular keeps, formidable though they were, had serious shortcomings. Any right-angled tower was necessarily weak at its angles, which were susceptible to mining and created 'blind spots' which the defenders could not command except directly from above. This led to the building of free-standing circular keeps, still with the entrance at first-floor level as with the right-angled keeps. Instances of such towers exist in France, Germany and England in the twelfth century but most of the surviving examples in England and Wales date from the early part of the thirteenth century. Of the known Welsh examples of the latter, about half are situated in the south, being concentrated mainly in Pembrokeshire, Breconshire, Monmouthshire and on the Herefordshire border. Incomparably the finest specimen in Wales is the 75 ft high tower built about 1200 by William Marshall within Pembroke Castle, a stronghold of exceptional importance at the time because it was being used as a base for expeditions designed to conquer Ireland. Smaller but excellent examples of the same technique can be seen at *Skenfrith*, where the round keep (diameter 24 ft) was set on the top of the motte, and at *Tretower*, where its three-storeyed tower (diameter 21 ft) was raised within an earlier shell keep. Others exist at *Bronllys* (Brecs.), Caldicot (Mon.) and just over the border at *Longtown* (Herefs.). This concentration of round keeps in South Wales at this time is thought to have been the result of the rivalries of the Marcher lords among themselves and of their concern at the growing power of Welsh princes, especially that of Llywelyn ab Iorwerth of Gwynedd, who was building castles of his own. At *Ewloe*, an outpost of Welsh power in Flintshire, there stands an interesting D-shaped keep which was very probably built at Llywelyn's orders, and at *Dolbadarn Castle*, another of his or his grandson's strongholds, there is a round keep of about 20 ft in diameter rising to 40 ft in height, which leaves no doubt of the mastery of the art of castle-building now being achieved by the Welsh rulers.

Thirteenth-century castles

The emphasis in thirteenth-century building, nevertheless, lay in the development not of the keep but of the bailey or curtain wall together with the adoption of the rounded mural or flanking tower. These wall towers brought to a number of separate points along the

Tretower Castle
White Castle

curtain-wall all the advantages of the round keep. Each tower was one of a series of self-contained strongholds which enabled the defenders to cover the outer face and base of the wall while remaining protected; each at the same time commanded the summit of the wall and divided it into sections, thus preventing a single break-in from endangering the whole castle. Some of the earliest of such towers were semi-circular and solid in their construction; but the merits of building them hollow so as to give extra accommodation and more fighting platforms were soon appreciated.

At *Chepstow*, as at Pembroke, the great William Marshall applied himself *c*. 1190 to bringing the defences up to date. He built the curtain-wall between the middle and lower bailey together with gateway and towers, the particular interest of which is that it is one of the earliest instances in England or Wales of rounded wall towers and the provision of true shooting slits. Marshall's son at *Cilgerran* built two round towers astride the curtain wall, thus facilitating a more aggressive form of defence. But the best impression of early castles using rounded towers to strengthen the curtain wall can be derived from *Grosmont* and *Skenfrith*, both of which are thought to have been reconstructed along these lines, probably between 1228 and 1232, by the Justiciar Hubert de Burgh, who held these lordships from 1219 to 1239.

Such towers in themselves were not enough. It was also essential to ensure the security of the entrance, always potentially the weakest point of the defences. This was achieved by building an increasingly powerful gatehouse which, in its earliest form, consisted of twin towers, usually D-shaped, on either side of the entrance. Admission to it across the ditch was gained by means of a bridge which pivoted on an axle rather like a see-saw, the gate-passage being defended by a series of defences, including a gate and portcullis and 'murder holes' in the vault overhead. Furthermore, the defenders could fire arrows into the gate-passage through slits from the chambers on either side. An early gatehouse still stands at *White Castle*, and another, partly ruined, at *Montgomery*, but a rather similar one at *Criccieth*, once thought to have been the work of Llywelyn ab Iorwerth, is now generally accepted to have been part of Edward I's reconstruction of that castle.

Later castle-building in thirteenth-century Wales reflects the fact that military and political power was being concentrated into fewer but more powerful hands. Thus, fewer Marcher lords ruled over a greater number of lordships. These lords were often locked in fierce rivalry with one another as well as with the King and the Welsh princes. Among the latter all others were eclipsed by the rise of Llywelyn ab Iorwerth (1194–1240) and Llywelyn ap Gruffudd (1247–

82). By the era of the second Llywelyn's adroit interventions in the wars between Henry III and his barons during the years from 1255–67, it became evident that any royal or Marcher castles but the strongest could be in jeopardy from the Welsh. It is no coincidence that round about this time, or shortly afterwards, major works should have been begun on what were to be some of the most power-ful castles in South Wales. *White Castle* was heavily refortified by the king's agents about the 1260s or 1270s; the inner ward at *Kid-welly* was built by Payn de Chaworth *c.* 1275; and, most significant of all, the castle at *Caerphilly*, one of the most superbly-conceived strongholds anywhere in medieval Europe, was begun by the strongest of the Marcher lords, Gilbert de Clare, possibly as early as 1268. Within the next decade Edward I had embarked on the programme of castle-building, unprecedented in scale and grandeur, which was intended finally to conquer Wales and to keep it con-quered.

In terms of medieval military architecture the pinnacle of achieve-ment was reached with the development of concentric castles in the last quarter of the thirteenth century. The concentric castle was provided with two sets of defences, one placed inside the other, and each complete in itself. On the inside was the four-sided inner ward, with its walls taken up to an immense height and protected at each corner by a drum tower and with its entrance or entrances sited between the towers and guarded by gatehouses and sometimes by barbicans as well. Surrounding this inner ward, only a matter of yards away, was the outer ward, also boasting a stout but lower curtain wall protected by round towers. In some instances a fortified town formed an integral part of the initial design, and its walls and guard towers ran outwards from the castle walls in an unbroken enclosure to form a single defended area.

Most of the concentric castles of Wales were built by the King, but at *Caerphilly* and *Kidwelly* in South Wales there are two notable examples built by Marcher lords. Caerphilly is, next to *Dover*, the largest castle in England or Wales and covers no less than 25 acres. At its heart is the inner ward, an irregular quadrangle of huge cur-tain walls, its two entrances reinforced by prodigious gatehouses, and its four corners protected by drum towers. Around this lies the outer ward with its relatively low battlemented walls designed to give a free field of fire from the inner ward. These two wards con-stitute the concentric castle proper but form only a part of the fortifications as a whole, being further protected by a series of intricate additional safeguards made up of inner and outer moats, lakes, earthworks and outer platforms. *Kidwelly Castle*, though much smaller, is aesthetically one of the most striking and pleasing

Caerphilly Castle

of all Welsh castles in conception. Here, the inner ward, dramatically crowning the steep ravine overlooking the River Gwendraeth, was built first. It protected the hall, solar, chapel (an unusually arresting feature in this castle) and other domestic buildings. So great was the natural strength of the ravine behind the inner ward that when, early in the fourteenth century, the outer ward with its formidable gatehouse came to be built, it needed only to be a semicircle, rather like a bow in design, and did not need to be taken round that part of the inner ward perched on the ravine.

The castle-building ambitions of the lords of the March, impressive though some of their results were, are dwarfed by the immensity of enterprise and planning represented in Edward I's castle-building programme in Wales. Between 1276 and 1296 he built no fewer than ten new castles of the first rank, remodelled three captured from the Welsh, renovated a number of older border strongholds, and inspired the building of four new lordship castles along the lines of those of his own creation.* So vast a scheme called for men,

*The ten new castles were *Flint*, *Rhuddlan*, Aberystwyth, Builth, Ruthin, Hope, *Conwy*, *Caernarvon*, *Harlech* and *Beaumaris*; the Welsh ones were *Dolwyddelan*, *Criccieth* and *Bere*; the border castles included Chester, Oswestry, Shrewsbury, *Montgomery* and St Briavel's; and the lordship castles were Hawarden, *Denbigh*, Holt and Chirk.

materials and money on a scale that taxed to the uttermost the abili-
ties of this most martial of English kings and the resources of his
prosperous kingdom, but in the end it secured permanent military
subordination of Wales. When Edward embarked upon it he was
already a seasoned warrior and strategist who had tasted war in
France and the Holy Land as well as in Britain. He was conversant
with the latest developments in the science of castle-building and
had had first-hand experience of the 'bastides', the planned fortress-
towns of southern France, and of their role in any design for conquest. Furthermore, he was able to take into his service Master
James of St George, a man who had already made a name for himself by building castles for the King's cousin, Philip, Count of Savoy,
and who was able to incorporate in the castles of North Wales the
perfected refinements of medieval military architecture. Edward's
castle-building in Wales falls into two stages in phase with his two
main campaigns there. The earlier opened in 1277. The king realized
that the border bases traditionally used for controlling Wales were
not sufficiently far advanced for his purpose, so he planned four new
forward bases at key-points in Mid and North Wales—Builth,
Aberystwyth, *Flint* and *Rhuddlan*. To build them, his agents recruited in the summer months of 1277 from a wide area in the Midlands and the West Country a huge labour force—at least 1845 diggers, 790 carpenters and 320 masons—who were put to work immediately, being given bonus payments when necessary but also
being subjected to stoppages for absenteeism. The outstanding
legacy of their work at *Flint Castle* is the great round tower known
as the 'donjon' which may possibly have been intended as a residence
for the royal Justice of Chester. Alongside the new castle at Flint
they also built a new town, planned like a French 'bastide' along the
sands of Dee, and protected by earthworks and palisade—hence the
army of diggers. *Rhuddlan*, too, got a new castle of concentric design
and a new town girdled with earthworks. But here a uniquely ambitious engineering feat was also undertaken, the course of the River
Clwyd being diverted for some two or three miles in order to provide
access to the sea. It took an average of 77 men working six days a
week three years to complete and the cost of castle, town and channel together was, in modern money, £1 million. Work on this first
stage of Edward's building went on from 1277 to the eve of the
Welsh revolt of March 1282. Indeed, the very timing of that revolt is
largely explicable in terms of Welsh alarm at the progress being
made on the castles, for there seems little doubt that the Welsh
struck when the intensive summer season of building was about to
begin.

Faced with the rebellion of 1282 Edward reacted promptly and comprehensively. Within a month of its outbreak, orders were being despatched to every part of England, to Ireland and Edward's lands in France for men and supplies of every kind. The speed and scale of that operation leave little doubt that Edward had already determined on a final reckoning with the princes of North Wales. When the latter's resistance failed in March 1283, opening the road to the heart of Gwynedd, Edward lost no time in laying the foundations of those new fortresses that were intended to keep the Welsh permanently under control. *Conwy* was begun in March, *Harlech* in April and *Caernarvon* in July. Meanwhile, Edward was urging his vassals to build similar castles of their own, like those at *Denbigh* and Chirk. That such bastions were needed was convincingly demonstrated by the dangerous Welsh uprising of 1294–95, led by Madog ap Llywelyn, which inflicted serious damage on *Caernarvon Castle* and led Edward to begin work on a new castle at *Beaumaris*. By the time of his death in 1307 most of Edward's work was completed, although building continued at Caernarvon until 1330, while at Beaumaris the upper storeys of all the towers and the inner part of the southern gatehouse were never finished.

The Edwardian castles, still so largely intact, constitute as a whole one of the most remarkable groups of medieval monuments to be seen anywhere in Europe. Their grandeur is in proportion to the money that had to be raised to build them and which had to be forthcoming regularly or else the work stopped, as it did for a time in Builth in 1277. Some £95–100 000, it has been reliably calculated on the basis of the royal records, was spent on Edward's castles in Wales between 1277 and 1330 and more than 80 per cent of that total was spent before 1301. *Caernarvon Castle*, *town walls* and quay and other buildings alone cost £27 000, *Conwy* and *Beaumaris* cost some £14–15 000, *Rhuddlan* about £9200. In so far as an equivalent in modern values can be given, the investment in these castles amounted to about £10 million and that at a time when the population of England and Wales was probably about one-twentieth of what it is now, and the gross national product infinitely smaller. The financial achievement was, therefore, as impressive as the feat of logistics achieved in recruiting the men and obtaining the supplies.

Castles in the later Middle Ages

After the Edwardian Conquest the military need for castles became less acute. Diminished threats led to greater negligence in upkeep. At *Conwy* as early as 1321 several of the roof trusses had failed and in 1332 it and other castles in North Wales were ruinous, as was *Cilgerran* in South Wales in 1326. A detailed survey carried out for

Rhuddlan Castle

the Black Prince in 1343 of his castles in Wales showed that many of them, including *Conwy* and *Beaumaris*, were in poor shape. Yet Welsh castles were, in general, less neglected than those in England, except for the ones on the northern border. This was because there were still considerable military risks along the periphery of the kingdom. The fourteenth century was one of constant warfare against Scotland and France, and there were repeated reports and rumours of the dangers of invasion. *Criccieth Castle*, for instance, was to be fully garrisoned and provisioned against invasion in 1338; one of Edward III's last acts in 1377 was to order *Cilgerran*, Tenby and Pembroke to be repaired and refortified; and in 1384–85 *Conwy* was on the alert because of 'persistent rumours touching war, rapine, murder and arson and the Scottish enemies'. Behind all the alarms lurked the greater fear that the Welsh might rise in support of any invasion. They did not do so on any scale, however, until the rebellion of Owain Glyndŵr in the first decade of the fifteenth century. When this was at its height only the strength of some of the castles stood between the rebels and the complete overthrow of English power in Wales. Among those which proved too strong and too well prepared to be taken were Brecon, *Chepstow, Rhuddlan, Conwy* (except for one brief episode) and *Caernarvon*, which withstood a long and desperate siege by Glyndŵr supported by his French allies. But a number of other castles were captured or severely damaged. Extensive and costly repairs had subsequently to be undertaken at

Conwy Castle
Harlech Castle

Ogmore, *Kidwelly*, Carmarthen and *Carreg Cennen*, described as 'lately completely destroyed and thrown down by rebels', while *Criccieth* was so badly damaged that it was abandoned. The rebels' greatest prizes were *Harlech*, which Glyndŵr for three years made his home and headquarters, and Aberystwyth. These two castles between them gave him control of large parts of western Wales.

Long after the rebellion had been suppressed, disturbed conditions persisted. They left an evocative monument in *Raglan Castle*, built by Sir William ap Thomas between about 1430 and 1445, and much extended by his son, William Herbert, the first Earl of Pembroke, from about 1450 to 1469. Its unique feature is its Great Tower, Tŵr Melyn Gwent ('Yellow Tower of Gwent'), which has no exact parallel anywhere else in Wales. Surrounded by water and cut off from the rest of the castle except for a drawbridge, it illustrates perfectly how the men of that age thought it necessary to have a self-contained fortified dwelling which could, if necessary, be held even against the owner's own retinue. Precautions of this sort were given added point by the rapid and brutal fluctuations of fortune and loyalty in the civil wars of the fifteenth century, in which contingents from Wales and the Marches played a considerable part. In such troubled times fears were expressed that a castle as strong as *Carreg Cennen* might become a bandits' lair to be exploited by 'all the misgoverned men' of the surrounding area who would live by 'robbery and spoiling of our people', and in 1462 they led to its being severely 'slighted' in order to avoid 'inconvenience of this kind happening there in the future'. In the north-west, *Harlech Castle* held out in Lancastrian hands for eight years and was the last castle to pass into the possession of the Yorkists.

In the sixteenth century stabler rule and a better ordered society were gradually established but the value of such castles as were used as centres of royal administration and justice increased rather than diminished after the Act of Union between England and Wales in 1536. It is not surprising to find in a survey of 1550 reporting on the state of *Monmouth Castle* a recommendation that repairs should be carried out on the grounds that the king had always had

> 'within the said Castle of Monmouth one place called the Exchequer where his auditors, receivers and other officers were wont to sit for hearing of matters, taking of his accounts and for receiving of his money; and now, by reason of . . . decays, they are driven to go into the town, which we think much unseemly.'

Other castles still inhabited by wealthy and powerful families were partially transformed into mansions where the accent was less on strength than ease, and more on luxury than security. Foremost among those who took advantage of the new possibilities in Wales

were the Somerset family, Earls of Worcester and unquestionably
the leading aristocratic family resident in the country. At their chief
seat in *Raglan*, the third earl (1548–89) began work on the splendid
hall, still the finest and least-decayed of the surviving apartments
there, and on the long gallery. These projects were completed by his
son, the fourth earl (1589–1628), who also added brick-built gazebos
or summerhouses and a series of statue niches, 'a pleasant walk set
forth with several figures of the Roman emperors in arches of diverse
varieties of shell-works'. The same family was responsible for contemporary modifications at *Chepstow*, where they enlarged the
windows and added a two-storey block of lodgings which has since
largely disappeared. *Oxwich Castle* in Gower was almost wholly
built by Sir Rhys Mansel (1487–1559), whose tall four-storey building with mullioned windows preserves fleeting shadows of its former
grandeur even in its present ruinous state. Less ruined and even
more magnificent is the work of Sir John Perrott (1530–92) at Carew
in Pembrokeshire, whose 'long line of graceful and entirely civilian
mullioned windows . . . is eloquent of the vanished military importance of the castle and its resultant transformation into a peaceful
and palatial country mansion'.*

Yet, in spite of all appearances to the contrary, the military importance of the castle had not finally vanished. When the civil war broke
out between King and Parliament in 1642, Wales was almost wholly
royalist, with a number of Welsh castles being used as major bases
in Charles I's cause. *Conwy Castle* was 'repaired, revictualled and
supplied with ammunition' for the king by one of the borough's own
sons, John Williams, archbishop of York (1641–50). *Caernarvon*,
three times closely besieged by the Parliamentarians, successfully
withstood their onslaughts, as did *Harlech*. Fighting was even harder
in south-east Wales, where, in the person of the Earl, later Marquis,
of Worcester, the King enjoyed the support of one of his wealthiest
and most loyal adherents. The Earl's castle at *Chepstow* was besieged
twice and his headquarters at *Raglan*, the most formidable royalist
stronghold in south-east Wales, endured in the summer of 1646 one
of the most hotly-contested and best-recorded sieges of the war. By
the end, the castle was being besieged by 3500 men under the command of Sir Thomas Fairfax himself, and when it finally surrendered
on 19th August 1646 the event was regarded by both sides as the
virtual ending of the First Civil War. In the Second Civil War in
1648 Pembroke Castle, the one great base in Wales which had held
out for Parliament throughout the First Civil War despite some very
strong and sustained pressure was, paradoxically, being held by
some of Cromwell's Presbyterian opponents. The great Oliver himself

---

*Brown, R. A. *English Medieval Castles*.

Caernarvon Castle
Beaumaris Castle

Caernarvon Castle

Beaumaris Castle

Raglan Castle
The Bishop's Palace, St David's

came to Pembrokeshire to conduct the siege that finally reduced this recalcitrant strongpoint. Neither here nor at *Raglan* had the use of gunpowder made a decisive difference, so powerfully constructed were the old stone defences. It was the subsequent 'slighting' which was ordered at both these castles and elsewhere, like *Flint* and *Rhuddlan*, that caused the real damage. Even then, at *Caernarvon*, where the inhabitants were entrusted with the responsibility for demolishing the defences, they found the task too laborious to justify the effort and expense involved.

Bishops' palaces and other buildings

In medieval Wales there were few landowners greater or wealthier than the bishops of St David's. As well as being princes of the Church they were, alone among the bishops of Wales, Marcher lords in their own right, owing allegiance to no secular lord but the King. They possessed rich and substantial estates widely scattered throughout south-western Wales, from which they drew an income about as large as that of the three other Welsh bishops combined. They were, in addition, guardians of the most famous and lucrative centre of pilgrimage in Wales, the shrine of David, first bishop and patron saint, two visits to which were popularly regarded as being the equivalent of one to Rome. Not surprisingly, therefore, these medieval successors to St David have left traces of their former wealth and status in more than one palace and castle. At St David's itself there survives a group of medieval buildings unsurpassed any-where in Wales. Around them run the remains of the medieval precinct walls with the sturdy and handsome twin-towered Porth y Tŵr ('Tower Gate') which dates from *c.* 1300. Enclosed within are not only the small but exquisite cathedral church with architectural features representing all major phases of medieval building but also the fourteenth-century college of St Mary (recently restored) and the *Bishop's Palace* itself.

The palace is very largely the handiwork of a succession of dis-tinguished builder-bishops who held the see in the thirteenth and fourteenth centuries. From the reign of Edward I (1272–1307) down to the beginning of the fifteenth century it was deliberate royal policy to plant in St David's bishops of the highest calibre who were also dependable agents of the Crown. Mostly men of ripe experience in Church and State, university graduates of more than ordinary stand-ing, they were administrators who stood high in the esteem of king and pope. The earliest of them was Thomas Bek (1280–93), a former chancellor of Oxford University and Lord Treasurer to Edward I in 1279. It was he who began work on the chapel, bishop's hall and solar, and the gatehouse, all in the eastern range of buildings. But the man who more than any other left his imprint decisively and characteristically on this palace was Bishop Henry Gower (1327–47). Scion of a noble South Wales family, an Oxford scholar of some note, and a public servant whose talents were widely employed by king and pope, this 'Welsh Wykeham' is nevertheless best known for his taste and enthusiasm as a builder, of which many testimonies still survive. The cathedral itself still bears the impress of his genius more strongly than that of any of its other builders, but Gower's finest monument is undoubtedly the Great Hall of the palace of St David's. Its most distinctive features are its arcaded parapets, which are also to be seen in other buildings attributable to Bishop Gower, notably in the palace at *Lamphey* and at *Swansea Castle*, which seems to have come into his possession for a time during the fourteenth century. Later additions to the palace may be the work of Bishop Adam Houghton (1361–39), who was, however, chiefly interested in St Mary's College, and of Bishop Edward Vaughan (1509–22) who also embarked upon building projects at the cathedral and at *Lamphey*. With the coming of the Reformation, however, the palace at St David's fell on evil days and was allowed by sixteenth- and seventeenth-century bishops to fall into decay.

Second only to the palace at St David's in interest is the bishop's residence at *Lamphey*, three miles to the east of Pembroke. Some of the buildings there—a hall and service rooms from the early-thirteenth century and a fine 'camera' or private apartment built perhaps by Bishop Richard Carew (1256–80)—are earlier than anything now surviving in the palace at St David's. However, Lamphey like St David's saw its days of greatest splendour under Bishop Gower. He built a new and larger hall there and remodelled the courtyard. His distinguishing mark is the use of the arcaded parapet, although at Lamphey many of the subtler touches associated with it are missing, which suggests that he may have had to be content with employing local craftsmen who were able to imitate the broad outline but could not reproduce the finer detail. Some further work of commendable quality was carried out at Lamphey in early sixteenth-century style, probably by Bishop Vaughan. Under Bishop William Barlow (1536–48), Lamphey was surrendered to Henry VIII in exchange for the rich rectory of Carew, and the palace and manor then passed from the King into the hands of the Devereux family, later Earls of Essex. The first and second earls both spent much of their youth at Lamphey, and there are signs of attempts to adapt the palace to the needs of the lay household of the Elizabethan period.

Llawhaden, the third of the major episcopal residences still surviving, is of very different character from the other two, being a castle rather than a palace. The estates here, too, were among the richest possessions of St David's diocese, and when the see passed under the control of the Norman bishops early in the twelfth century a ring-motte castle with earth and timber defences was built to protect these alien prelates. This castle, destroyed by the Welsh in 1192, may have been rebuilt in stone during the thirteenth century, but it was not until the beginning of the fourteenth century that it was reconstructed on its present lines as the work of Bishop David Martin (1293–1328), himself of Marcher stock and deeply involved in the political and military tensions of the period. Bishops' registers show that *Llawhaden*, like *Lamphey*, continued to be much used by bishops and their representatives throughout the fourteenth and fifteenth centuries down to the Reformation. At that stage, however, *Llawhaden* was very largely abandoned in favour of the bishop's palace at Abergwili near Carmarthen.

Monastic buildings

BROADLY speaking, there were four kinds of buildings found within the average monastery: (i) the church; (ii) the claustral buildings in which the monks lived; (iii) buildings in which they dispensed hospitality or charity; and (iv) buildings in which they exercised routine management of their estate and other administrative business.

The church

This was the very heart of the monastery. It was here that the monks carried out their essential vocation of the service of God by means of prayer, praise and worship. Monastic churches were therefore designed to enable monks to carry out the 'Opus Dei' ('service of God'). They were nearly all cruciform in shape, and where they were not, as in *Cymmer Abbey*, this was only because circumstances had prevented the carrying out of the original design. Many of the churches were very large: Margam, for instance, was 262 ft long and $63\frac{1}{2}$ ft. wide; *Tintern* was 228 ft long and *Neath* 223 ft. Some other churches were laid out on a grand scale which it was found impossible to complete; *St Dogmael's* and *Cymmer* because of the troubles caused by warfare, and *Talley** because of a long and costly quarrel with Whitland.

The best surviving example of an early monastic church in Wales is at *Ewenny*. The nave, with its single north aisle, has the immense circular pillars and rounded arches of the early Norman style, which must presumably date from the original foundation of the priory early in the twelfth century. In monastic times it was used by the

---

*A house of Premonstratensian canons.

parishioners for worship. The crossing, presbytery and transept, which were the monks' preserve, are of more elaborate Norman workmanship and were probably built in the late twelfth century. Although there is some later rebuilding and though the north transept has virtually disappeared, Ewenny gives a more vivid impression of what a Norman church was like than any other in Wales. At *St Dogmael's*, unlike Ewenny, Christian worship has not survived in the original monastic church, which has long been ruinous; and also unlike Ewenny, the church at St Dogmael's underwent considerable modification in the thirteenth and fourteenth centuries. Even so, enough of the earliest work survives at St Dogmael's to enable us to tell what the original church plan was like in the first half of the twelfth century. It, too, was cruciform, with an aisled nave, and it had a short presbytery, probably with an apse at the eastern end. Each of the transepts also had an apse at its eastern end, the outline of which can still be seen in the south transept.

The original twelfth-century Cistercian church was uncompromisingly simple in plan, as befitted an Order which laid such emphasis on austerity and the absence of ornament. A good example of such a design has been discovered by excavation at *Tintern*, slightly to the north of the site of the later church and overlapping it. Shorter, much narrower and simpler than its successor, this early church consisted of an aisle-less nave, short transepts with rectangular chapels on the east side, and a short, aisleless, square-ended presbytery. The essentials of this early plan still survive at *Valle Crucis* even though it was not founded until 1201. Here, although the nave is aisled, the presbytery and both transepts are short and square-ended. The Cistercian church at *Basingwerk*, built early in the thirteenth century, shows the same 'family likeness' to Valle Crucis which tended to characterize Cistercian building. The growing wealth and success of the Cistercian Order during the thirteenth century, coupled with the tendency for more monks to enter the priesthood and so to need more altars, led to a number of their churches being rebuilt on a grander and more elaborate scale. At *Strata Florida* the addition was relatively modest and involved no more than extending the presbytery eastward by about 20 ft. But at *Neath* and *Tintern*, in the late thirteenth and early fourteenth century, the church was rebuilt with an aisled presbytery having a series of chapels at the east end behind the high altar, aisled north and south transepts with chapels at the east end, and an aisled nave. Much of Tintern's magnificent church with its ambitious proportions, graceful vaulting and traceried windows still stands, and it illustrates clearly how far the White Monks had moved away from their founders' notions of simple and unostentatious austerity.

The nave in the Cistercian churches was reserved for the use of the 'conversi' or lay-brothers. These were monks who took vows of poverty, obedience and chastity, but whose chief function was to cultivate estates, tend livestock and look after buildings belonging to the monastery. They often outnumbered the choir monks in the early days of Cistercian monasteries when the Order was developing hitherto uncultivated or deserted land. The aisles of the nave were shut off by solid stone screens to form the lay-brothers' quire, traces of which remain at *Strata Florida* and *Tintern*. The monks' quire covered the crossing and sometimes extended into the easternmost bay of the nave, where a stone screen known as a pulpit ummarked the division. On Sundays and on certain holy days the abbot and his monks went in solemn procession visiting all the altars in the church and making a ceremonial round of all the claustral buildings. Later Cistercian churches like those at *Neath* and *Tintern* covered the west door with a small but elaborate porch known as a 'Galilee', so called because the abbot leading his monks in procession was thought to symbolize Christ leading His disciples into Galilee.

The claustral buildings

The buildings in which the monks lived were grouped round three sides of a cloister, with the church itself forming the fourth side. The cloister was ordinarily placed on the south side of the church to catch the sun, but where other considerations, like those of drainage, dictated, it was sited on the north side of the church, as at *Tintern*. It was usually placed against the nave of the church, but there are examples—*Penmon* is one—of the cloister being set against the chancel of the church. The cloister consisted of four covered passageways or walks, with lean-to roofs, set round a square garth or courtyard. The walls had open arcades or, later, windows looking out on to the courtyard. Doors gave access from the cloisters to the range of buildings on each of its sides, thus providing a covered way between the church and all parts of the monastery. It was in the cloister, also, that a monk was expected to spend much of his time reading and meditating. This was generally done in the cloister walk next to the church; and halfway along this walk at *Tintern* can be seen the remains of the canopied seat occupied by the abbot during the Collation, the reading before Compline, while at *Strata Florida* the position of the lectern used in the Collation can still be traced.

In considering the claustral buildings of smaller Welsh abbeys and priories it must be remembered that many of these houses had never, at best, had more than the minimum provision. The eastern range usually consisted of a two-storey block, with the whole of the first floor forming the 'dorter' or dormitory of the monks, although at

Tintern Abbey
Llanthony Priory

Llanthony it appears that they slept in the upper storey of the western range and at *Penmon* in the southern range. There was always direct communication between the dorter and the 'rere-dorter' or latrine block, the site of which was determined by the position of the main drain and the adequacy of the water supply needed to flush it. At *Valle Crucis* the rere-dorter lay immediately south of the dorter and in direct line with it; at *Tintern* it lay at right angles to the dorter; while at *Neath* it was placed parallel to the dorter and was connected to it with a bridge. Access from the dorter to the church was usually gained by means of night stairs which led into the south transept. A moulded handrail of such night stairs survives at *Neath*, and at *Ewenny* a newel staircase; but at *Llanthony*, perhaps because the dorter was in the western range, there appears to have been no direct communication between it and the church.

On the ground floor of the eastern range next to the transept there was, in early plans, a passage called a 'slype', which still exists at *Llanthony*. But in rather later Cistercian plans there was a narrow room serving as a sacristy where the vessels used in the church were stored. This was the arrangement at *Basingwerk*, *Strata Florida*, *Valle Crucis*, and *St Dogmael's*; but the same room might be used as a library and vestry, as at *Neath* and *Tintern*. The next room in this range was the chapter house, which came second only to the church in importance and was so called because it was there that the monks assembled each day after morning mass to hear a chapter of the Rule read and to discuss the business of the house. Early chapter houses were square or rectangular buildings with three bays, like the one at *Valle Crucis*, the west end of which was used as a library and contained a book closet. But because of its importance the chapter house was very often enlarged and made more ornate in later extensions. It was remodelled and extended at *Basingwerk* and *Strata Florida;* at *Tintern* it was rebuilt on much ampler lines with richly decorated doorways; and at Margam one of the loveliest and most elegant chapter houses anywhere in Britain was built in polygonal shape with intricate vaulting springing from a central pillar. Beyond the chapter house the ground floor of the eastern range might be used for a variety of purposes, including novices' lodgings (*Basingwerk* and *Tintern*), an inner parlour (*Basingwerk* and *Tintern*) or a warming-house (*Basingwerk* and *Penmon*)—the only place in the monastery, except the kitchen, in which a fire was permitted.

In the range opposite the church, which might be north or south depending on the position at which the cloister had been set, the chief room was the 'frater' or dining-hall of the monks. It usually had an entrance on the west side, near which was a lavatory where the monks washed their hands before meals. At meal-times one of the monks ascended to read a chapter from the scriptures from the frater pulpit, remains of which are still in evidence at *Basingwerk* and *Tintern*. The earliest frater ranges were built along the length of the cloister opposite the church, as can be seen at *St Dogmael's Llanthony*, and *Cymmer*. But this plan was markedly altered in later Cistercian arrangements whereby the frater was set at right angles to the cloister and projected well beyond the main walls of the range (*Tintern, Valle Crucis* and *Basingwerk*). This change made it possible to build a warming-house east of the frater and parallel with it. It also meant that the kitchen placed to the west of the frater could serve both its needs and those of the lay-brothers' frater which lay in the western range of buildings.

The western range of buildings in Benedictine houses contained the cellar or great storehouse of the monastery, so placed because the outer court, which was the outlet to the world, lay on the west side. The only other room that was invariably placed on the west side was the public parlour (*Llanthony, St Dogmael's* and *Tintern*), which formed an entrance between outer court and cloister where conversation between monks and lay-people could take place. In Cistercian monasteries, however, the western range of buildings was given over to 'conversi' or lay-brothers for their frater and dorter (*Neath* and *Tintern*). This meant that the abbot's house and the guests' lodgings, which in Benedictine houses like *St Dogmael's* were in the west range, had usually to be located elsewhere in Cistercian houses.

Other buildings

The 'farmery' or infirmary, where monks who were sick or very old were cared for, usually lay to the east of the cloister (*Basingwerk, St Dogmael's* and *Tintern*). It had its own hall and chapel and oftentimes its own frater and kitchen as well. At *Tintern* they formed a sizeable block of buildings which shared a second cloister, the infirmary cloister, with the dorter and rere-dorter range.

In the outer court to the west of the cloister buildings there might be a whole miscellany of structures. These could include the guests' lodgings where the abbot or prior, like any other great landowner, could entertain. The prior of Carmarthen, for example, was reported as having had complimentary messages from the King of Portugal acknowledging his hospitality to Portuguese merchants. Also in the outer court, at appropriate points, there might be a variety of humbler buildings, many of them of wood, housing workshops, livestock or stores. In the same area, near the gateway, would stand the almonry, at which the poor and sick foregathered to receive charity dispensed by the almoner. The main gatehouse through which the monastery was entered was often a handsome two-storeyed

affair, as can be seen at *Llanthony* or *Neath*. More than one gatehouse was needed where the precinct was extensive, *eg* at *Tintern*,
where the precinct wall enclosed 27 acres and was entered by a number of gates including a water-gate on the Wye. The outstanding
precinct wall in Wales, however, is the one at *Ewenny*, complete with
two impressive gates, stoutly-built towers, and a splendidly-pre-
served wall with battlements and a wall-walk in places. But it is not,
as it is often said to be, an authentic example of a fortified ecclesiastical building since the battlements and towers are largely for display. On the vulnerable east side, where heavy defences would have
been most needed, the simple precinct wall remained unfortified
throughout the Middle Ages.

Disintegration and Dissolution of the Monasteries

THE religious Orders had passed their peak by 1300—no new houses
were subsequently founded in Wales and those in existence had
already begun to show signs of declining vitality. During the next
two centuries they faced a succession of difficulties and crises. Long
wars with France led to heavy taxation and to the cutting off of
contacts with mother houses in France, including Cîteaux. The
Black Death of 1348–49 and later visitations of plague caused a
sharp reduction in the number of choir monks and made recruitment
difficult afterwards; the Cistercian lay-brothers virtually disappeared
from the scene. Labour shortages and other economic troubles made
it wellnigh impossible for the monks to cultivate their estates and
they had no choice but to rent them out to laymen. To add to the
monks' misfortunes came the Glyndŵr rebellion, which caused
havoc and devastation in many parts of Wales. In 1402, *Strata
Florida* was occupied by royal troops, its monks expelled and its
buildings desecrated. *Talley* by 1410 was said to have been 'de-
spoiled, burned and almost destroyed', and Margam in 1412 to be
in such a bad state that its abbot and monks were obliged to wander
around like vagabonds. *Ewenny* and *Llanthony* also suffered grievous
losses. One small Welsh priory, the Benedictine cell at Cardiff,
actually disappeared during the troubles, and a Cistercian house,
Abbey Cwm-hir, was so badly affected that it was never more than a
shadow of itself again.

It took a long time for the other Welsh monasteries to recover from
this succession of adversities. In some respects they never really
regained their former vitality. The complement of monks in practically every house remained persistently below strength; *Tintern* alone
among Welsh houses seems to have had the thirteen monks regarded
as the necessary minimum. The quality of monastic life tended to

deteriorate—a monastery became less a community than a collection of individuals, and abbots, on whom the temper of life within the monastery chiefly depended, frequently built or adapted for themselves elaborate private lodgings in which they lived in comparative luxury. At *Valle Crucis*, for instance, there was a succession of three abbots of whom we know a fair amount: John ap Richard (*c.* 1450–80), Dafydd ab Ieuan (d. 1503) and John Lloyd (elected 1503). All three were liberal patrons of Welsh poets, who describe with admiration the energy and money which these abbots, and especially the first two, put into their building projects. But the main features of this fifteenth-century reconstruction do not speak very highly of the spirit prevailing in the monastery at the time. Only the eastern part of the church was being used, the nave being no longer required as there were now no lay-brothers. The eastern walk of the cloister was also abandoned and the northern part of the dorter and the room above the sacristy adapted to provide a hall and chamber, complete with fireplace, for the abbot. New provisions for the abbot of the same general kind were made at *Neath* and Aberconway, less certainly at *Basingwerk*, and probably elsewhere as well.

Yet in the last resort it was not the decay of the monasteries which led to their final dissolution by Henry VIII between 1536 and 1539, so much as the political and financial needs of the Crown. But it was their decline which probably prevented any outcry against their closure, which was carried through in Wales without provoking any serious disturbance. Once the monasteries had been closed the fate of their buildings varied widely. Most of the churches belonging to the Benedictine Order or the Orders of canons, having previously been used for worship by layfolk continued in use as parish churches, and Brecon Priory church has in this century attained the status of a cathedral. However, at *Talley* in the eighteenth century and *St Dogmael's* in the nineteenth, new parish churches were built to take the place of the old ones. The Cistercian churches, sited in lonelier and less populated places and not having served as parish churches, suffered heavily. The lead was soon removed from the roofs of many of them and melted down for the King's use; lead from *Basingwerk* was used at Holt Castle and even transported as far as Ireland to repair the royal castles at Dublin and elsewhere; but at *Tintern* a good deal of the lead was bought by the Earl of Worcester, to whom the site and many of the abbey's estates were granted. Stone and timber might also be removed for the King's benefit, as at Aberconway, whence they were transported to *Caernarvon* to repair the castle. Margam proved to be a rare exception among Cistercian churches; its church was truncated, and the nave only was afterwards used for parish worship as, indeed, it still is.

Conventual buildings, other than churches, in many instances disappeared completely or were incorporated into houses, farms, or other buildings on or near the monastic site. This was especially true of the Benedictine and Austin canons' houses situated in busy towns. The same fate usually befell the friaries of the Dominicans and Franciscans although two of them, Brecon and Bangor, became adapted as schools, and a third, the Grey Friary, at Cardiff, which was modified to make a town house for a branch of the Herbert family, has disappeared only within the last few years. *Ewenny's* buildings were also incorporated into a private residence for a family of gentry and they have been continuously inhabited ever since. Part of *St Dogmael's* western range became adapted as a rectory and was used for that purpose for a long time. A number of other monasteries were used as residences for lay-folk—*Strata Florida, Valle Crucis* and *Basingwerk*—but have for centuries been uninhabited, while the site of *Neath Abbey* was occupied first by a Tudor mansion and subsequently by an iron foundry. Even now, in ruins, they retain much of their attraction. It is still possible to understand why John Leland described *Neath* as having been 'the fairest abbey in all Wales', or why the white-robed Cistercians of *Valle Crucis* once appeared to a medieval poet, Gutun Owain, as the very harbingers of Heaven itself.

The Industrial Revolution

by D. MORGAN REES, MA, FSA

THE fact that Wales lies in the so-called Highland Zone of Britain has played as important a part in its industrial development as in its social and political history, for its uplands contained the raw materials required by industry while in early times its woods provided fuel and its rivers power.

Strictly speaking the history of industry in Wales goes back almost to the arrival of the first men, and there is still visible evidence of industry—metalliferous mining in particular—of Roman and other early periods in many parts of Wales. None the less it is reasonable to regard the second half of the sixteenth century as the starting point for modern industrial growth. From this time on there are comparatively substantial remains of industrial activities in Wales and owing to rapidly increasing interest in industrial archæology these can now be protected by the State as Ancient Monuments in the same way as prehistoric and medieval sites. The remains are principally associated with the making of iron, the mining of coal and metals and with the quarrying of slate, as well as with the communications essential to the exploitation of these resources.

Ironmaking

In three areas in Glamorgan (one near Bridgend, the others in the river valleys of the Taff and Aman) and in the Wye Valley in Monmouthshire there are remains of small sixteenth and seventeenth century ironmaking blast furnaces built of stone. These used as raw material iron ore from outcrops, as fuel charcoal made from local timber supplies and as power the waters of rivers and streams to drive the waterwheels which operated the blast-giving bellows and tilt hammers. In counties no longer associated with ironmaking, such as Carmarthenshire, Pembrokeshire, Cardiganshire and Montgomeryshire there are ruins of stone furnaces and forges established during the early years of the eighteenth century on locations which were in easy reach of timber supplies.

The industrial upsurge, which began during the second half of the eighteenth century and continued into the nineteenth resulted in the building of numerous ironworks along the northern rim of the South Wales Coalfield. These benefitted from the discovery of coke-making from coal and from the use of steam engines. On many of these sites, and in other parts of South Wales, there remain the ruins of stone blast furnaces and associated buildings.

An interesting example of an eighteenth-century charcoal furnace—probably the best preserved in Great Britain—is on the river Einion in the Cardiganshire village called Furnace. A map, which appeared in a book by William Waller describing the silver and lead mines of Cardiganshire published in 1699, indicated that the site was first occupied by silver mills which had five smelting furnaces. The building from its present barnlike appearance is seen to have had a complicated structural history, but whatever may have been its original state it was converted into an ironmaking blast furnace in 1755. As a blast furnace it had the usual square stack emerging from the roof, a feature which disappeared when it ceased operations after 1814, and clinging to its east wall there was a cast house into which the molten iron flowed from the furnace after it had been tapped. There remain faint traces of this building in the wall.

This site is known as the Dovey Furnace and many features associated with furnaces of the period remain; for example, the charging floor connected to the natural rock bank and on the same level part of the upper section of the furnace complete with a charging hole for the iron ore and charcoal, this hole being in the form of a Gothic arch. At ground level the housing for the bellows which provided the blast can be entered and the arched entrance to the fore-hearth remains, but the furnace lining and the crucible have been removed and it is now possible to stand inside the furnace looking upwards to the roof of the present building. On the west wall there are parts of a waterwheel which—when it was operative—was driven, as was the wheel which operated the blast-providing bellows, by water running along a leat from the nearby river.

The working of furnaces on two levels was a normal feature at sites such as Dovey. From the second half of the sixteenth century until, in some cases, the first half of the nineteenth century, such ironmaking blast furnaces, with outer walls made of stone, were built into sloping ground. This resulted in the furnace charge hole and its charging platform being at a higher ground level to make for easier charging of the raw materials.

Among the best examples of the furnaces of the late eighteenth century, now ruined but illustrating this principle, are those at Blaenavon, Monmouthshire. This ironworks dated from 1789. In 1799 there were three blast furnaces and by 1814 two more had been added. The present remains show some interesting features such as the round shape of one of the stacks and the brick courses which formed it, reinforcement rods made of iron and the walls of a cast house jutting out from the front of a pair of furnaces. There is also on the site the shell of the structure of a water balance tower which was used to take up iron ore from ground level to the upper level where the raw materials were prepared and afterwards charged into the furnaces. This was built when imported ore came to Blaenavon by rail.

In close proximity to the works there once stood a number of streets and a tenement at one time owned by the company. In recent years all have been demolished with the exception of Stack Square which is, however, in a ruinous condition.

Coalmining

After 1830, in Glamorgan and Monmouthshire, the coal industry ceased to be subsidiary to the iron industry and for the remainder of the nineteenth century there was rapid development in the sinking of pits. The growing coal industry, in the same way as the iron industry, benefitted considerably from the increased use of steam engines which were used for a variety of purposes including pumping and winding.

Since the early years of the coal industry, winding head-frames above shafts, and engine houses which contained the steam winding engines, have been familiar features on colliery surfaces. A typical engine house is being preserved on the site of the former Elliot Colliery, East Pit, New Tredegar, Monmouthshire. It was built in 1891 and the winding machinery which is still in the building, was originally a twin simple engine, but was later enlarged to form a twin tandem compound arrangement.

Metalliferous mining

In most Welsh counties there are surface remains of different kinds, which were connected with mining of silver, lead and zinc, for copper and for gold. The gold used for royal wedding rings has been mined in Wales. Cardiganshire and Montgomeryshire, during the nineteenth century particularly, provided the greatest number of lead mines, and the remains of engine houses, water-courses, water-wheel pits, and occasionally waterwheels, are still to be seen. Among these are the surface ruins of *Bryntail Lead Mine*, three miles north-west of Llanidloes, at the foot of the Clywedog Dam. This was the first Industrial Monument to be taken into guardianship in Wales. A lease for the mine was first granted in 1770, but its most productive period for lead ore was between 1845 and 1867 when nearly 2000 tons were mined. Two leats, an upper and lower, carried a supply of water from the Clywedog River at a point to the north-west of the site. It is reasonably obvious that the upper leat carried the water at a level above and behind the surface buildings to a waterwheel outside a crusher house—the original wheel-pit is still recognizable as such despite its present ruined condition. Much of the gable end

of the main building remains and there are ruinous retaining walls
built into the bank which rises to the north-east of the site and
other walls in a similar condition which suggest that there were
other buildings nearby used for ore dressing purposes.

The open mouth of a pumping shaft is a feature of the site; this is
situated directly in line with a ruined waterwheel pit from which
pump actuating rods ran along a culvert, now fallen in, to the bell
crank which worked the pumping rods in the shaft. At a point near
the river's edge there is the mouth of an adit level into which the
water from the bottom workings was probably pumped to drain
away into the river.

The ruins of an ore bin made of stone adjacent to those of bridge
abutments on each side of the lower leat indicate the carriage of ore
down an incline from a level near the hill top to the dressing floor
area.

For a period of nearly 50 years after 1867 the mine was worked for
barytes, a mineral which may have been crushed by millstones, parts
of which still remain and two of which have been recovered intact.
The mineral was mostly worked in the upper parts of the mine and
brought down for crushing on the incline. The remains of slate tanks
suggest that after crushing it was chemically treated—probably
bleached—and as excavation work has revealed the existence of
small ovens and earthenware vessels it is concluded that the crushed
barytes was dried after recovery from the tanks before being carted
away from the site for further processing at a factory. A ruined
engine house suggests the introduction of a steam-engine during
this period.

Slate quarrying

This has been described as the most Welsh of Welsh industries, but
for a number of years the slate quarries of North Wales have been
closing down. Among the most recent of these is the Dinorwic
Quarry, near Llanberis, which closed in 1969 after nearly 200 years
of working. Three thousand men were at one time employed in the
great quarry, which rises in steplike terraces for 1400 ft above the
waters of Llyn Peris and which was once the biggest slate quarry in
the world. The workshops which serviced and maintained the quarry
were housed nearby in pleasing stone and slate buildings, surrounding a spacious quadrangle. These contained many kinds of machine
tools, blacksmiths' hearths, wood-working machines, an iron foundry and a large waterwheel which until 1925 provided power
throughout the complex. The workshops and their contents are

being developed into a museum for the slate industry with the addition of redundant machinery from other quarries.

The first stage of the North Wales Quarrying Museum was opened in May 1972. The foundry has been laid out to give it the appearance of a working foundry and the cupola, in which the pig iron was melted before casting, and its charging platform have been suitably restored. Of the original ten blacksmiths' hearths, four have been retained to make up one smithy, which contains a large number of tongs and the shaping tools used. The fitting shops have on display old machine tools including different kinds of lathes, slotting machines and drilling machines. Slate dressing is featured in a section containing slate sawing tables, slate dressing machines and hand tools. The waterwheel, 50 ft 5 in. in diameter, 80 horse-power, installed in 1870, to drive the entire transmission machinery is one of the museum's chief attractions. A short length of the quarry railway which formerly carried the slate down to Port Dinorwic is also being restored and preserved.

Roads, canals and railways

There is no doubt that the demands of ironmasters of the late eighteenth and early nineteenth centuries, and afterwards the coal owners, were responsible for the first developments in means of transport and communication to meet industrial needs. When the early ironmasters began to establish themselves there were no roads worthy of the name. Finished iron, and coal, were taken from the developing valleys to the ports by mule troops. It is said that the first road was completed by Anthony Bacon in 1767, with the assistance of local farmers, from Merthyr Tydfil to Cardiff, through Caerphilly. This road, which soon became difficult to use, was followed by a turnpike road which ran along the floor of the Taff Valley. It was used to take wagon-loads of iron to Cardiff. Such turnpike roads were frequently maintained by the levying of tolls, and many toll-houses are still to be seen at the roadside, particularly in North Wales. One outstanding example, complete with toll-gates and list of tolls, is preserved in the Welsh Folk Museum at St Fagans.

The early roads did not give the ironmasters the links which they wanted with the ports. Canals were, therefore, built very quickly at the end of the eighteenth century—the Glamorgan Canal, the Monmouthshire Canal, the Neath Canal, the Brecon and Abergavenny Canal (extending the Monmouthshire Canal), the Swansea Canal—and others followed. The ironworks and the coal mines were linked to the canals by many miles of tramroads and the canals carried enormous tonnages between the works and the ports. There remains a great deal of evidence of the canals and tramroads—most of the Brecon and Abergavenny Canal is navigable and in use, and miles of tramroads are marked by lines of stone sleepers placed at regular intervals in the ground and by occasional cast-iron bridges. This applies to North Wales as well as South Wales; the Pont Cysyllte aqueduct carrying the Ellesmere Canal survives as an outstanding example of its kind.

In South Wales after 1840 the rapid growth of the coal industry demanded increased means of transport which was satisfied by a remarkable network of railways. The Taff Vale Railway between Cardiff and Merthyr was opened in April 1841. There followed many railways bearing the names of famous railway companies such as the Rhymney, Barry, Brecon and Merthyr, Rhondda and Swansea Bay, which ultimately became the Great Western Railway Company. The railway needs of mid-Wales were met during the second half of the nineteenth century. The quarries of North Wales were linked to such ports as Portmadoc by narrow-gauge railways, some of which remain today only as traces to be followed and inclines to be recognized, while others (such as the Ffestiniog, Llyn Padarn and Talyllyn Railways) have been re-opened for the enjoyment of summer visitors. The swiftness of the revolution in transport from need to closure had been startling. The homely signal box is already an obsolete relic in many parts of Wales, while the survival of bridges, viaducts and other major railway engineering works will increasingly depend on their intrinsic merit as industrial monuments.

It is hoped that in due course Dovey Furnace, the Blaenavon iron works, the engine-house at Elliot colliery and the buildings which now house the North Wales Quarrying Museum at Dinorwic (all described above) will be placed in the guardianship of the Secretary of State.

Conversion Table

FEET	METRES	YARDS	METRES
1 ft	0·3 m	30 yd	27·4 m
5 ft	1·5 m	35 yd	32·0 m
10 ft	3·0 m	40 yd	36·6 m
15 ft	4·6 m	45 yd	41·1 m
20 ft	6·1 m	50 yd	45·7 m
25 ft	7·6 m	100 yd	91·4 m
30 ft	9·1 m	200 yd	182·9 m
35 ft	10·7 m	300 yd	274·3 m
40 ft	12·2 m	400 yd	365·8 m
45 ft	13·7 m	500 yd	457·2 m
50 ft	15·2 m	1000 yd	914·4 m
100 ft	30·5 m		
		1 acre	0·4 hectare
1 yd	0·9 m	5 acres	2·02 hectares
5 yd	4·6 m	10 acres	4·05 hectares
10 yd	9·1 m		
15 yd	13·7 m	1 mile	1·60 km
20 yd	18·3 m	5 miles	8·04 km
25 yd	22·9 m	10 miles	16·09 km

Further Reading

General

BOWEN, E. G., and GRESHAM, C. A., *History of Merioneth* Vol. 1. Dolgellau. 1967.

HOULDER, C. and MANNING, W. H. *Regional Guide to the Archaeology of South Wales*. London. 1966.

LLOYD, SIR J. E. *History of Wales from the Earliest Times to the Edwardian Conquest*. Cardiff, 3rd ed. 1939.

MOORE, D. (ed.). *The Irish Sea Province in Archaeology and History*. Cardiff. 1970.

REES, W. *An Historical Atlas of Wales from Early to Modern Times*. London, 3rd ed. 1967.

ROYAL COMMISSION. *Inventories of Ancient Monuments* (Anglesey, Caernarvonshire, Carmarthenshire, Denbighshire, Flintshire, Glamorgan (in preparation), Merioneth, Montgomeryshire, Pembrokeshire, and Radnorshire). H.M.S.O.

SORRELL, A. *Living History*. London. 1965. (With reconstruction drawings.)

WATSON, K. *Regional Guide to the Archaeology of North Wales*. London. 1965.

Prehistory

DANIEL, G. E. *Prehistoric Chambered Tombs of England and Wales*. Cambridge. 1950.

FOSTER, I. LL. and DANIEL, G. E. (ed.). *Prehistoric and Early Wales*. London. 1965.

FOX, SIR CYRIL. *Life and Death in the Bronze Age*. London. 1959.

GRIMES, W. F. *The Prehistory of Wales*. National Museum of Wales. 1959.

LYNCH, F. *Prehistoric Anglesey*. Llangefni. 1970.

PIGGOTT, S. *Ancient Europe*. Edinburgh. 1965.

POWELL, T. G. E. (ed.). *Megalithic Enquiries in the West of Britain*. Liverpool. 1969.

The Roman Occupation

BARNETT, C. *Handbook to the Roman Caerwent Collection*. Newport Museum and Art Gallery. 1969 ed.

BOON, G. C. *Isca*. National Museum of Wales. 1972.

BOON, G. C. and WILLIAMS, C. *Plan of Caerleon-Isca*. National Museum of Wales. 1967.

COLLINGWOOD, R. G. and RICHMOND, SIR IAN. *The Archaeology of Roman Britain*. London. Revised ed. 1969.

CRASTER, O. E. *Caerwent Roman City*. H.M.S.O., 1971 ed.

DANIELS, C. M. and JONES, G. D. B. 'The Roman Camps on Llandrindod Common', *Archaeologia Cambrensis*. 1969.

DAVIES, R. W. 'Roman Wales and Roman Military Practice-Camps', *Arch. Camb.* 1968.

FRERE, S. S. *Britannia: a History of Roman Britain*. London. 1967.

JARRETT, M. G. and MANN, J. C. 'The tribes of Wales', *Welsh History Review*. Vol. 4.

JONES, G. D. B. and LEWIS, P. R. *The Roman Gold Mines at Dolaucothi*. Carmarthen County Museum Publication No. 1, 1972 (guidebook).

MOORE, D. *Caerleon, Fortress of the Legion*. National Museum of Wales. 1970. (Guidebook for schools).

NASH-WILLIAMS, V. E. *The Roman Frontier in Wales*. 2nd. ed. revised under the direction of M. G. Jarrett, Cardiff, 1969.

OGILVIE, R. M. and RICHMOND, SIR IAN (ed.). *Cornelii Taciti de Vita Agricolae*, (Appendix IV for summary of Roman metal production). Oxford. 1967.

RIVET, A. L. F. *Town and Country in Roman Britain*. London, Revised ed. 1964.

RIVET, A. L. F. *The Roman Villa in Britain*. London. 1969.

WATSON, G. R. *The Roman Soldier*. London. 1969.

WEBSTER, G. *The Roman Imperial Army of the First and Second Centuries* A D London. 1969.

Early Christianity and the Dark Ages

BOWEN, E. G. *The Settlement of the Celtic Saints in Wales*. Cardiff. 1956.

BOWEN, E. G. *Saints Seaways and Settlements*. Cardiff. 1969.

FOSTER, I. LL. and DANIEL, G. E. (ed.). *Prehistoric and Early Wales*. London. 1965.

FOX, SIR CYRIL. *Offa's Dyke, a Field Survey of the Western Frontier Defences of Mercia in the Seventh and Eighth Centuries*. Cardiff. 1955.

JACKSON, K. H. *Language and History in Early Britain*. Edinburgh. 1953.

JAMES, J. W. *Rhigyfarch's Life of St David*. Cardiff. 1967.

JONES, F. *The Holy Wells of Wales*. Cardiff. 1950.

NASH-WILLIAMS, V. E. *The Early Christian Monuments of Wales*. Cardiff. 1950.

WADE-EVANS, A. W. *Vitae Sanctorum Britanniae et Genealogiae*. Cardiff. 1944.

The Middle Ages

COLVIN, H. M. (ed.). *History of the King's Works*. Vols. I and II, London. 1963.

GRESHAM, C. A. *Medieval Stone Carving in North Wales*. Cardiff. 1968.

HOGG, A. H. A. and KING, D. J. C. 'Early Castles in Wales and the Marches', *Arch. Camb.* 1963 'Masonry Castles in Wales and the Marches', *ibid.*, 1967. 'Castles in Wales and the Marches: Additions and Corrections', *ibid.*, 1971.

RENN, D. F. *Norman Castles in Britain*. London. 1968.

SIMPSON, W. D. *Castles in England and Wales*. London 1969,

WILLIAMS, G. *The Welsh Church from Conquest to Reformation*. Cardiff. 1962. See also *Castles* and *Abbeys* published by HMSO.

The Industrial Revolution

DODD, A. H. *The Industrial Revolution in North Wales*. Cardiff. 3rd edn., 1971.

HUDSON, K. *Industrial Archaeology—an Introduction*. London. 1963.

LEWIS, W. J. *Lead Mining in Wales*. Cardiff. 1962.

NORTH, F J. *Mining for Metals in Wales*. Cardiff. 1962.

RAISTRICK, A. *Quakers in Science and Industry*. Newton Abbott. 1968.

REES, D. M. *Mines, Mills and Furnaces, an Introduction to Industrial Archaeology in Wales*. London. 1969.

REES, W. *Industry before the Industrial Revolution*. Cardiff. 1968.

SCHUBERT, H. R. *History of the British Iron and Steel Industry from 450 BC to AD 1775*. London. 1957.

Castell Coch

Notes

THE following list of monuments cared for by the Department of the Environment on behalf of the Secretary of State for Wales includes a brief description of each monument and a note on its location. Admission times are given when these differ from the standing hours. Map references relate to the O.S. one-inch maps of Great Britain, seventh series.

Admission

Standard hours of admission

	Weekdays	Sundays
March, April, October	9.30 am—5.30 pm	2 pm—5.30 pm
May—September	9.30 am—7 pm	2 pm—7 pm
November—February	9.30 am—4 pm	2 pm—4 pm

Most major monuments are also open on Sunday mornings from April to September inclusive from 9.30 am. All monuments are closed on Christmas Eve, Christmas Day and Boxing Day.

Entry is free at monuments marked on the list with an asterisk(*). Elsewhere admission fees are charged ranging from 5p upwards. Children under sixteen years of age and pensioners are admitted at reduced prices. Visiting parties of eleven or more can obtain a discount of 10 per cent on the total admission fee on application to the custodian.

Season tickets

Season tickets, valid for a year from the date of issue, admit their holders to all ancient monuments and historic buildings in the care of the State. Tickets can be purchased at many monuments; at HMSO bookshops; from the Ancient Monuments Division, Department of the Environment, Gabalfa, Cardiff CF4 4YF; and from the Department of the Environment (AMHB/P), 25 Savile Row, London W1X 2BT. Full information will be supplied on request.

Publications

Guidebooks, postcards and colour slides are on sale at many monuments. Full lists of the items available can be obtained on application to the London office of the Department at the address given above, or to HMSO at the addresses given on the back cover.

Photography

Photographs may normally be taken by visitors for their own use but the use of tripods and other stands for cameras is at the discretion of the custodian. The taking of photographs for commercial purposes is forbidden without a permit. Applications for such permits should be made to the Ancient Monuments Division, Department of the Environment, Gabalfa, Cardiff CF4 4YF. Large prints of official photographs of most monuments may be obtained at commercial rates from the Photographic Library, Department of the Environment, Hannibal House, Elephant and Castle, London SE1.

Anglesey

See *Official Guide to Ancient Monuments of Anglesey*, obtainable (price 15p) at Beaumaris and Caernarvon Castles, or direct from HMSO at addresses on back cover.

Barclodiad y Gawres Burial Chamber, Aberffraw*
A megalithic passage grave in which five of the stones are ornamented with spirals and incised lines.
Situation: Close to the sea, 2 miles north-west of Aberffraw. Map sheet 106, ref. SH 328707.
Admission: Temporarily closed. Access by prior arrangement with the Superintendent of Works, Ancient Monuments Division, 22–23 The Square, Caernarvon (Caernarvon 3094).

Beaumaris Castle
Last-founded of the great castles of the Edwardian conquest and the finest example of the concentrically planned castle in Britain.
Situation: In Beaumaris. Map sheet 106, ref. SH 607763.

Bodowyr Burial Chamber, Llanidan*
A cover stone supported on three uprights with possible traces of the mound.
Situation: Near Bodowyr farm, 1¼ miles east of Llangaffo. Map sheet 106, ref. SH 462681.

Bryn Celli Ddu Burial Chamber, Llanddaniel-Fab*
A chambered burial cairn of *c.* 2000 BC, overlying an earlier sanctuary of henge type consisting of a ditch and circle of stones.
Situation: ¾ mile east-south-east of Llanddaniel-Fab. Map sheet 106, ref. SH 507701.
Admission: Temporarily closed. Access by prior arrangement with the Superintendent of Works, Ancient Monuments Division, 22–23 The Square, Caernarvon (Caernarvon 3094).

Caer Lêb, Llanidan*
An earthwork comprising originally two banks and two ditches enclosing an area 200 ft by 160 ft. Discoveries in this area suggest occupation in the third century AD or later.
Situation: ¾ mile west-north-west of Bryn Siencyn. Map sheet 106, ref. SH 473675.

Caer y Twr, Holyhead Rural*
A hill fort with single stone rampart, in places 10 ft high. The rampart walk and parapet are visible on the east side. Its precise date is uncertain.
Situation: On the summit of Holyhead Mountain. Map sheet 106, ref. SH 219829.

Capel Lligwy*
Remains of small twelfth-century chapel, rebuilt in the fourteenth and enlarged in the sixteenth century.
Situation: ¾ mile north of Llanallgo. Map sheet 106, ref. SH 499863.

Castell Bryn-gwyn, Llanidan*
A defensive site of the Neolithic period, twice rebuilt and altered, latterly in the first century AD.
Situation: 1¼ miles west of Bryn Siencyn. Map sheet 106, ref. SH 465670.

Din Dryfol Burial Chamber, Aberffraw*
The remains of a megalithic passage grave on an unusual site.
Situation: 350 yards south-east of Fferam-dryfol farm. Map sheet 106, ref. SH 395724.

Din Lligwy*
A well-preserved walled hut group comprising remains of two circular and seven rectangular buildings. Dates from the fourth century and may perhaps have been the headquarters of a local chieftain.
Situation: ¾ mile north-north-west of Llanallgo. Map sheet 106, ref. SH 497861.

Holyhead Mountain hut circles*
A native village of the Roman period. A well-preserved collection of huts, mostly circular but some rectangular.
Situation: On the south-west slope of Holyhead Mountain 500 yards north-west of Tŷ Mawr. Map sheet 106, ref. SH 211819.

Holyhead Roman Fort (Caer Gybi)*
Part of the wall of the fort, on the north and west sides of St Cybi's churchyard, is in the Secretary of State's guardianship; it dates from the late third or early fourth century.
Situation: Holyhead. Map sheet 106, ref. SH 247826.

Lligwy Burial Chamber, Penrhos-Lligwy*
A good example of a megalithic burial chamber. The capstone, weighing about 28 tons, is supported by low upright stones over a natural fissure in the rock. Remains of thirty individuals were found in the chamber.
Situation: ½ mile north of Llanallgo. Map sheet 106, ref. SH 501861.

Penmon Cross*

An elaborate carved stone cross with rectangular shaft and circular head, dating from about AD 1000.
Situation: ¼ mile west-north-west of priory church. Map sheet 107, ref. SH 626808.

Penmon Dovecot*

Fine square dovecot of *c.* 1600, with domed vault and hexagonal cupola.
Situation: 100 yards south-east of priory church. Map sheet 107, ref. SH 631807.

Penmon, priory buildings*

These comprise the south range (thirteenth century) and southern end of the west range (sixteenth century) of the claustral buildings of the Augustinian priory. The former contains the refectory, with the dormitory above and a cellar below; the latter was probably the prior's lodging with kitchen and guest hall, and has since been adapted as a dwelling (not accessible).
Situation: 3½ miles north-north-east of Beaumaris. Map sheet 107, ref. SH 630807.

Penmon, St Seiriol's Well*

Believed to have been used in the sixth century by St Seiriol; the well-chamber is largely rebuilt but the circular hut nearby may be the remains of the saint's cell.
Situation: 80 yards north-north-east of priory church. Map sheet 107, ref. SH 631808.

Penrhos Feilw Standing Stones, Holyhead Rural*

Two stones 10 ft high and 11 ft apart, presumably set up in prehistoric times.
Situation: 100 yards north-west of Plas Meilw. Map sheet 106, ref. SH 227809.

Presaddfed Burial Chamber, Bodedern*

Two megalithic chambers, 7 ft apart, possibly originally in a long cairn.
Situation: 300 yards west-south-west of Presaddfed. Map sheet 106, ref. SH 347809.

Trefignath Burial Chamber, Holyhead Rural*

A fine example of the 'segmented cist' type, with a passage once divided by cross-slabs into three or four chambers.
Situation: 1½ miles south-south-east of Holyhead. Map sheet 106, ref. SH 258805.

Tregwehelydd Standing Stone, Llantrisant*
A single stone, 8½ ft high.
Situation: ⅓ mile north-west of Tregwehelydd farmhouse. Map
sheet 106, ref. SH 341832.

Tŷ-mawr Standing Stone, Holyhead Rural*
A single stone, nearly 9 ft high.
Situation: 600 yards north-west of Trefignath farm. Map sheet
106, ref. SH 253809.

Tŷ-newydd Burial Chamber, Llanfaelog*
A massive cover stone rests on three uprights; there is no certain
trace of the mound. Bronze Age relics have been recovered from
the chamber.
Situation: ¾ miles north-east of Llangaelog church. Map sheet 106,
ref. SH 344738.

Breconshire

Brecon Gaer*
A Roman fort founded *c.* AD 75 rebuilt in stone during the mid-
second century, and later abandoned. Part of the fort walls on the
north-east (standing to a height of 11 ft) as well as the foundations
of the gateways on the west, south and east are in the Secretary
of State's guardianship.
Situation: 2¾ miles west-north-west of Brecon, near the village of
Aberyscir. Map sheet 141, ref. SO 004296.
Admission: Access restricted whilst the hay crop is standing during
the months of May, June and July.

Bronllys Castle*
A very fine early thirteenth-century round tower standing on top
of a twelfth-century castle mound.
Situation: ¾ mile north-west of Talgarth and 7 miles south-west
of Hay. Map sheet 141, ref. SO 149348.

Tretower Castle
Cylindrical keep of the early thirteenth century, standing within
the remains of an earlier rectangular structure, the whole apparently covering a low motte. The bailey is occupied by a farmyard,
but its thirteenth-century curtain wall is in the Secretary of State's
charge.
Situation: 150 yards west of Tretower Court. Map sheet 141, ref.
SO 184214.

Tretower Court
>One of the finest surviving medieval houses in Wales, mainly of the fifteenth century. Considerable alterations were carried out about 1630.
>*Situation:* 2½ miles north-west of Crickhowell. Map sheet 141, ref. SO 184214.

Caernarvonshire

Caernarvon Castle
>The most important of the Edwardian castles, and from 1284 to 1536 the administrative centre of North Wales. The first defence of the site was an earthern motte-and-bailey, made by the Normans between 1088 and 1098 and subsequently occupied by the Welsh princes. The present castle was begun in 1283.
>*Situation:* In Caernarvon. Map sheet 106, ref. SH 477626.
>(Official guidebook includes Town Wall.)

*Caernarvon Town Wall**
>The wall was for the defence of the free borough established in 1284. After the revolt of the Welsh in 1294–95 it was repaired at a cost of over £1000. Almost the entire circuit remains to the level of the wall-walk.
>*Admission:* No admission to wall tops.

Caernarvon, Segontium Roman Fort
>The most important Roman auxilliary fort in North Wales. The northern half has been excavated, and many of the finds are displayed in the museum on the site.
>*Situation:* On the outskirts of Caernarvon, on the Beddgelert road (A487). Map sheet 106, ref. SH 485624.

Conwy Castle
>Built by Edward I between 1283 and 1289 to command the Conwy ferry on the main coastal road into Snowdonia. A magnificent example of medieval military architecture.
>*Situation:* In Conwy. Map sheet 107, ref. SH 784774.
>(Official guidebook includes Town Wall.)

Conwy Town Wall
>Built contemporaneously with Conway Castle to enclose the English borough founded in 1284. The wall, with its 27 towers and 3 main gateways, is the most perfect example of its date now surviving in Britain.
>*Admission:* To part of wall only.

Criccieth Castle

A native Welsh castle dating mainly from the first half of the thirteenth century. Major alterations were made by Edward I, who founded a borough and included Criccieth in the general garrison scheme of the North Wales coast.

Situation: In Criccieth. Map sheet 116, ref. SH 500377.

Dolbadarn Castle

A Welsh castle, of which the principal remains are a massive round tower of the early thirteenth century. Finely situated on rocky hill, commanding the entrance to the Llanberis Pass.

Situation: ½ mile south-east of Llanberis. Map sheet 106, ref. SH 586598.

Dolwyddelan Castle

One of the castles of the princes of Gwynedd (North Wales) with a well-preserved rectangular keep probably dating from the middle of the thirteenth century.

Situation: 1 mile west of Dolwyddelan village. Map sheet 107-116, ref. SH 721523.

Admission: Closes on Sundays at 4 p.m.

*Ffynnon Gybi (St Cybi's Well)**

A well-chamber of very primitive construction, largely dry-built but of late date.

Situation: 1 furlong north-west of Llangybi church, which lies 4¾ miles north-east of Pwllheli. Map sheet 115, ref. SH 427413.

Gwydir Uchaf Chapel

The chapel built in 1673, was the private chapel of Gwydir House. It is notable for its painted ceiling of contemporary date, and for its original gallery and fittings.

Situation: ½ mile south-west of Llanrwst. Map sheet 107, ref. SH 794609.

*Penarth Fawr**

The hall, screens and buttery of a house probably built by Madoc of Penarth, who was living in 1416. The remains of the screen are a fine example of 'spere' construction, in which a high timber arch is carried up to the level of one of the main roof trusses.

Situation: 3 miles north-east of Pwllheli. Map sheet 115, ref. SH 419376.

Cardiganshire

Strata Florida Abbey

Remains of church and cloister of Cistercian abbey founded in 1164.

Situation: 1¼ miles south-east of Pontrhydfendigaid, 14 miles south-east of Aberystwyth. Map sheet 127, ref. SN 746657.

Carmarthenshire

Carreg Cennen Castle
> The castle of late thirteenth-century date consists of a single court-yard surrounded by curtain wall and towers; of the original outer ward only foundations remain.
> *Situation:* 3¼ miles south-east of Llandeilo. Map sheet 140, ref. SN 668190.

Kidwelly Castle
> Originally founded during the reign of Henry I. The earthwork defences belong to this period. The rectangular inner ward was built *c.* 1275, the chapel being an addition of *c.* 1300. The outer curtain was built early in the fourteenth century. The town gate is also in the care of the Secretary of State.
> *Situation:* In Kidwelly. Map sheet 152, ref. SN 409071.

*Llanstephan Castle**
> A picturesque castle standing above the mouth of the River Towy. The remains, which include a great keep-gatehouse, are mainly of the late thirteenth century. There are extensive ditches, some of which date from the foundation of the castle by the Normans at the beginning of the twelfth century.
> *Situation:* 8 miles south-west of Carmarthen. Map sheet 152, ref. SN 352102.

Talley Abbey
> The abbey was founded towards the end of the twelfth century, probably by Rhys ap Gruffydd, for Premonstratensian canons.
> *Situation:* In the village of Tally, 6½ miles north of Llandeilo. Map sheet 140, ref. SN 632327.

Denbighshire

*Capel Garmon Burial Chamber, Llanrwst**
> A long cairn of 'Cotswold-Severn' type, containing a triple burial chamber.
> *Situation:* ¾ mile south of Capel Garmon village. Map sheet 107, ref. SH 818544.

*Chirk Castle Gates**
> Ornamental wrought-iron gates and screen made in 1719–21 by the brothers Robert and John Davies of Bersham, near Wrexham. Before 1770 they stood on north front of Chirk Castle.
> *Situation:* At the Chirk entrance to Chirk Castle Park. Map sheet 117, ref. SJ 281377.

Denbigh Castle

Built between 1282 and 1322 by Henry de Lacy, Earl of Lincoln, and his successor, for the defence and domination of the surrounding district. Refortified and garrisoned for the king during the Civil War, when it withstood a six-months' siege.
Situation: In Denbigh. Map sheet 107, ref. SJ 051657.
(Official guidebook includes all Denbigh monuments.)

Denbigh Friary*

Remains of the quire of a church of Carmelite friars, ruined since its destruction by fire in 1898. The building is of the early fourteenth century, the tracery of the east window being an insertion of *c.* 1400.
Situation: On eastern outskirts of town. Map sheet 108, ref. SJ 059666.

Denbigh, Leicester's Church*

The outer walls of an unfinished church began in the second half of the sixteenth century by Robert Dudley, Earl of Leicester, and said to have been intended to supplant the cathedral church of St Asaph.
Situation: On the lower side of Castle Green. Map sheet 118, ref. SJ 053659.
Admission: Exterior only.

Denbigh, St Hilary's Chapel*

Surviving tower of chapel built *c.* 1330 and described in 1334 as 'the chapel within the walls'. Remainder of building demolished in 1923.
Situation: On the lower side of Castle Green. Map sheet 108, ref. SJ 052659.
Admission: Exterior only.

Denbigh Town Wall

Contemporary with the foundation of the borough in 1282; the eastern salient is an addition of the early fourteenth century. Most of the enceinte is still traceable and the Burgess Gate is intact.
Admission: Key from Denbigh Castle.

Derwen Churchyard Cross*

A decorated stone pillar cross dating from the fourteenth or fifteenth century. The niches on the head contain sculptures of God the Father enthroned, the Crucifixion, and the Judgment of Souls.
Situation: On south side of church; Derwen is $4\frac{1}{2}$ miles north of Corwen. Map sheet 108, ref. SJ 070507.

Eliseg's Pillar, Llantysilio-yn-Ial*
  The most famous inscribed stone in Wales. It was erected in the
  ninth century AD for Prince Cyngen of Powys, who died at Rome
  in AD 854, to the memory of his great-grandfather Eliseg. It bears a
  long inscription, now illegible.
  Situation: ¼ mile north of Valle Crucis Abbey. Map sheet 116,
  ref. SJ 203445. (A guide pamphlet is obtainable at Valle Crucis
  Abbey.)

Valle Crucis Abbey
  The remaining buildings, for the most part dating from the
  thirteenth century, comprise the abbey church, sacristy, chapter
  house and, on the upper floor of the eastern range, the monks'
  dorter. The abbey was founded in 1201 for Cistercian monks by
  Madog ap Gruffydd, prince of Powys.
  Situation: 1½ miles north-west of Llangollen. Map sheet 108-117,
  ref. SJ 205442.

Flintshire

Basingwerk Abbey*
  Founded as a house of the Savignac Order in 1131 and subsequently transferred to the Cistercians. There are extensive remains
  of the conventual buildings, with the south transept and lower
  courses of the south and west walls of the church, mostly of the
  thirteenth century.
  Situation: ¼ mile south of Holywell Junction Station. Map sheet
  108, ref. SJ 196774.

Ewloe Castle
  An example of a native Welsh castle with typical round and
  apsidal towers. At least two successive building periods, both of
  the thirteenth century, can be distinguished.
  Situation: 1 mile north-west of Hawarden. Map sheet 109, ref.
  SJ 288675.

Flint Castle
  Built by Edward I between 1277 and 1284 and planned, with the
  town, like a continental bastide. Remarkable for its donjon or
  great tower, which is mentioned in Shakespeare's Richard II.
  Situation: In Flint. Map sheet 108, ref. SJ 247733.

Maen Achwyfan, Whitford*
  A fine wheel-cross of the eleventh century, with characteristic
  interlacing ornament on all four sides.
  Situation: 1 mile west north-west of Whitford church. Map sheet
  108, ref. SJ 129788.

Rhuddlan Castle
> An imposing example of a concentric castle of simple design, begun by Edward I in 1277. The castle commands the once important anchorage in the estuary of the Clwyd and the crossing of the river by the main coast route into North Wales.
> *Situation:* In Rhuddlan. Map sheet 108, ref. SJ 024779.

Rhuddlan, The Twthill*
> A large earthen mound, the motte of the castle built in 1073 by order of William the Conqueror.
> *Situation:* On east bank of River Clwyd, close to Rhuddlan Castle. Map sheet 108, ref. SJ 026776.

St Winifred's Chapel, Holywell*
> The well and chapel were built *c*. 1500 on the traditional site of the martyrdom of St Winifred (seventh century), probably replacing an earlier medieval shrine. The upper chapel only is in the guardianship of the Secretary of State.
> *Situation:* Immediately west of Holywell parish church. Map sheet 108, ref. SJ 185764.
> *Admission:* Exterior only during repairs.

Glamorgan

Bridgend, Newcastle Castle*
> A small castle dating from the twelfth century. On the south side a rectangular tower adjoins a remarkable Norman entrance gate.
> *Situation:* ½ mile north-west of Bridgend Station. Map sheet 154, ref. SS 902801.

Caerphilly Castle
> A concentrically-planned castle of the late thirteenth and early fourteenth centuries, notable for its great scale and use of water defences.
> *Situation:* In Caerphilly, 6 miles north of Cardiff. Map sheet 154, ref. ST 155871.

Castell Coch
> A small medieval castle, formerly ruined, restored in 1875 by William Burges for the 3rd Marquis of Bute with lavish interior decoration.
> *Situation:* Above Tongwynlais, 5 miles north-west of Cardiff. Map sheet 154, ref. ST 131826.

Coity Castle

The inner ward contains a square keep of late twelfth-century date. Other buildings in this ward, together with the outer ward, belong to the fourteenth century, which saw an almost complete rebuilding of the castle.

Situation: 1½ miles north-east of Bridgend. Map sheet 154, ref. SS 923816.

Ewenny Priory*

The priory was established in 1141 by Maurice de Londres, lord of Ogmore, as a cell of the Benedictine abbey of St Peter's, Gloucester. The buildings in the care of the Secretary of State include the transept and vaulted chapel of the priory church (mid-twelfth century) and the fortified precinct wall and gateways (late twelfth and early thirteenth centuries).

Situation: 1½ miles south of Bridgend. Map sheet 154, ref. SS 912778.

Admission: Work in progress: free admission, at the discretion of the owner, during working hours.

Loughor Castle*

Single tower of the late thirteenth or early fourteenth-century date, with traces of adjacent curtain wall on site of earlier earthwork castle commanding crossing of River Loughor. Overlies Roman fort of Leucarum.

Situation: In Loughor, south of main Swansea-Llanelly road (A484). Map sheet 153, ref. SS 564980.

Margam Stones Museum

Contains an important collection of inscribed and ornamented stones, mostly pre-Norman in date and all found in the locality; now housed in the old school-house.

Situation: North side of Margam Churchyard. Map sheet 153, ref. SS 801864.

Hours of admission: March–October: Wed., Sat. and Sun. 2 pm–5 pm; November–February: Wed., Sat. and Sun. 2 pm–4 pm.

Neath Abbey

Ruins of Cistercian (originally Savignac) abbey founded by Richard de Grainville in 1130. There are considerable remains, dating principally from the thirteenth century, of the west front of the church and of the claustral buildings.

Situation: 1 mile west of Neath, to south of main Neath-Swansea road (A48). Map sheet 153, ref. SS 738975.

Neath Abbey Gatehouse*

Fragment of building which may have formed part of main gateway to the abbey precinct.

Situation: On north side of main Neath-Swansea road, 1 mile west
of Neath. Map sheet 153, ref. SS 737976.
Admission: Exterior only.

Ogmore Castle and stepping stones

The castle has an inner and an outer ward, each surrounded by a
moat; the former is enclosed by a stone curtain of early thirteenth-
century date and contains a twelfth-century rectangular keep.
Situation: 2½ miles south-west of Bridgend. Map sheet 154, ref.
SS 882769.

Old Beaupre Castle*

A ruined medieval manor house, largely remodelled in the sixteenth century; the gatehouse (1586) and the porch (1600) are
especially notable.
Situation: 2 miles south-south-east of Cowbridge. Map sheet 154,
ref. ST 009721.

Parc le Breos Burial Chamber*

One of the best preserved passage graves in Wales, built in Neolithic times for the communal burial of the dead.
Situation: Gower peninsula, ½ mile north-west of Parkmill, 7 miles
west south-west of Swansea. Map sheet 153, ref. SS 538898.

St Lythan's Burial Chamber*

Impressive remains of megalithic chambered tomb, with massive
capstone supported on three uprights; probably dating from the
Neolithic period (*c.* 2500 BC).
Situation: 6 miles south-west of Cardiff, ¾ mile south-west of
village of St Lythan's. Map sheet 154, ref. ST 100722.

Swansea Castle*

The remains are still much engulfed by later buildings which will
be removed. The castle's finest feature at present visible is the
magnificent arcaded parapet dating from the first half of the
fourteenth century which recalls those at St David's and Lamphey.
Situation: In the centre of Swansea on the east side of Castle
Square. Map sheet 153, ref. SS 657931.
Admission: Exterior only.

Tinkinswood Burial Chamber*

One of the largest and best preserved chambered tombs in Britain,
of Neolithic date (*c.* 2500 BC).
Situation: 6 miles west-south-west of Cardiff, ½ mile south of
village of St Nicholas. Map sheet 154, ref. ST 092733.

Weobley Castle

A medieval fortified manor house; the hall and the kitchen wing date from the second half of the thirteenth century, the solar, the gatehouse range and the chapel being additions of the early part of the following century.

Situation: Gower peninsula 11 miles west of Swansea. Map sheet 152, ref. SS 478927.

Hours of admission: April–September, *weekdays* 10 am–7 pm; *Sundays* 1 pm–7 pm; October–March, *weekdays* 10 am–4 pm; *Sundays* 1 pm–4 pm.

Merioneth

Castell y Bere*

Extensive remains of a native Welsh castle, probably begun by Llywelyn ap Iorwerth in the third decade of the thirteenth century, and added to at the time of the English conquest (*c.* 1285).

Situation: Near the village of Llanfihangel-y-Pennant, 6½ miles north-east of Towyn. Map sheet 116, ref. SH 667086.

Cymmer Abbey

Remains of the church of a small Cistercian monastery dating from the earlier years of the thirteenth century.

Situation: 1¼ miles north-west of Dolgellau. Map sheet 116, ref. SH 721195.

Dyffryn Burial Chamber*

Two separate burial chambers set in a long cairn.

Situation: 5 miles south of Harlech. Map sheet 116, ref. SH 589228.

Harlech Castle

Built by Edward I between 1283 and 1290. A good example of the concentric plan, full development of which can be seen at Beaumaris. It is well preserved and very finely situated.

Situation: In Harlech. Map sheet 116, ref. SH 581313.

Llangar, Old Parish Church*

Small, aisleless, medieval parish church with structural alterations and internal features (pews, two-decker pulpit, fragmentary wall-paintings) of later date.

Situation: 1 miles south-west of Corwen. Map sheet 117, ref. SJ 064424.

Admission: Exterior only while under repair.

Monmouthshire

Caerleon Roman Amphitheatre
The only Roman amphitheatre in Britain which has so far been completely excavated. It was constructed during the last twenty years of the first century AD.
Situation: On the south side of Caerleon, 2 miles north-east of Newport. Map sheet 155, ref. ST 338903.

Caerleon, Prysg Field (*remains of the Roman Legionary Fortress*)
The fortress was laid out in about AD 75. The remains include a stretch of the fortress-defences, a latrine and the foundations of four long rectangular barrack-buildings (three are modern).
Situation: 2 miles north-east of Newport, on west side of Caerleon. Map sheet 155, ref. ST 337906.

Caerwent Roman City*
The Roman town of Caerwent was the cantonal capital of the Silures. The town wall is among the best-preserved of Roman date in Britain, and has added towers. The greater part of the wall is in the custody of the Secretary of State, as are also the foundations of a temple, and a house and shop in Pound Lane dating from *c*. AD 100.
Situation: 5 miles south-west of Chepstow. Map sheet 155, ref. ST 470905.

Chepstow, Bulwarks Camp*
A large earthwork, typical of a number which occur on the south coast of Wales. It relies in part upon the natural defence of a cliff. It probably dates from just before the Roman conquest.
Situation: 1 miles south of Chepstow. Map sheet 155, ref. ST 538927.

Chepstow Castle
A fine and extensive ruin, embodying buildings of most centuries from the Norman conquest to the Civil War. The lower part of the great hall is among the earliest buildings of its kind in the country.
Situation: On the west bank of the Wye, close to Chepstow Bridge. Map sheet 155, ref. ST 533941.

Chepstow, Port Wall*
Town wall, with attached towers, of thirteenth-century date, marking the extent of the medieval borough which it formerly enclosed. Originally continuous from Chepstow Castle on north to River Wye on east, and still intact for the greater part of its length.
Admission: Visible from ground only, no access to wall tops.

Grosmont Castle*

The castle consists of a single ward surrounded by a deep moat.
The buildings were largely erected by Hubert de Burgh, who held
Grosmont from 1201–43: additions were made in the first half of
the fourteenth century.

Situation: 2 miles south-south-east of Pontrilas, and 9 miles
north-east of Abergavenny. Map sheet 142, ref. SO 405244.

Hen Gwrt, Llantilio Crossenny*

Medieval moated house site, with rectangular enclosure still surrounded by wet moat.

Situation: ¼ mile east-north-east of Llantilio church, at corner of
road to White Castle, 6 miles east of Abergavenny. Map sheet 142,
ref. SO 396151.

Llanmelin Wood Camp*

Hill fort of the pre-Roman Iron Age, with triple bank and ditch
defences, a complex annexe and a small, embanked satellite earthwork on a nearby rise.

Situation: 1¼ miles north-west of Caerwent. Map sheet 155, ref.
ST 461925.

Llanthony Priory*

Founded *c.* 1108 for Augustinian canons. The present buildings
date from the first quarter of the thirteenth century. The ruins
comprise the greater part of the church and cloisters. The west
claustral range is in private occupation.

Situation: 9 miles north of Abergavenny. Map sheet 142, ref. SO
289278.

Monmouth Castle*

The principal remaining building is a rectangular two-storey block
of twelfth century date (with considerable alterations of *c.* 1340)
containing the hall of the Norman castle.

Situation: On a cliff above River Monnow, close to centre of
Monmouth. Map sheet 142, ref. SO 507129.

Monmouth, Great Castle House*

Built in 1673, within the ward of the older castle. Contains good
woodwork and an exceptionally fine decorated plaster ceiling.
Occupied by the Monmouth County Territorial Association.

Situation: Adjoins Monmouth Castle. Map sheet 142, ref. SO
507129.

Admission: Exterior only.

Newport Castle*

The remains comprise the eastern and most important part of a
once extensive structure of the Usk. Three towers, lined by a
curtain wall, are preserved. Date: early fifteenth century and later.

Situation: On the right bank of the Usk beside Newport Bridge. Map sheet 155, ref. ST 312884.
Admission: Free admission at discretion of local authority.

Raglan Castle
Extensive and imposing remains of fifteenth-century castle with moated hexagonal keep. After prolonged siege, surrendered to Parliamentary forces in August 1646 and was subsequently dismantled.
Situation: 6½ miles south-west of Monmouth and ½ mile north of Raglan village. Map sheet 155, ref. SO 415083.

Runston Chapel*
A small ruined chapel of early twelfth-century date, standing on the edge of a deserted village settlement.
Situation: 3 miles south-west of Chepstow, east of the Crick-Shire Newton road. Map sheet 155, ref. ST 495916.

Skenfrith Castle*
A National Trust property placed in the guardianship of the Secretary of State. A round keep is surrounded by a thirteenth-century curtain wall with towers at intervals.
Situation: 6 miles north-north-west of Monmouth. Map sheet 142, ref. SO 457202.

Tintern Abbey
Founded for monks of the Cistercian Order in 1131. Very extensive remains of the fine church (thirteenth century) and conventual buildings.
Situation: 5 miles north of Chepstow. Map sheet 155, ref. SO 532998.

White Castle
The castle consists of inner and outer wards. The stone defences of the former are of late twelfth and early thirteenth-century date.
Situation: 5 miles south-south-east of Abergavenny. Map sheet 142, ref. SO 380168.

Montgomeryshire

Bryntail Lead Mine*
Remains of nineteenth-century industrial buildings and stone settling-tanks formerly associated with processing of ore from nearby mine.
Situation: At the foot of the Clywedog dam, 3 miles north-west of Llanidloes. Map sheet 128; ref. SN 913868.

Dolforwyn Castle, Bettws*

The remains of a castle built by Llywelyn ap Gruffydd in 1273; not yet excavated.

Situation: 3¼ miles north-east of Newtown, off the Welshpool road. Map sheet 128, ref. SO 152950.

Montgomery Castle*

Remains of a castle built by Henry III in 1223–27, and later associated with the Herbert family.

Situation: Overlooking Montgomery. Map sheet 128, ref. SO 221967.

Pembrokeshire

Carew Cross*

A large pre-Norman inscribed cross of early eleventh-century date, with free wheel-head and tall shaft, decorated with panels of carved interlacing ornament.

Situation: Near entrance to Carew Castle, 4 miles north-east of Pembroke. Map sheet 138-151, ref. SN 047037.

Cilgerran Castle

A National Trust property placed in the guardianship of the Secretary of State. Substantial remains of castle of mid-thirteenth-century date. The site, a promontory of great natural strength above the gorge of the River Teifi, was occupied by the Normans as the administrative centre of the lordship of Emlyn from early in the previous century.

Situation: At west end of Cilgerran village, 2 miles south-east of Cardigan. Map sheet 139, ref. SN 195431.

Lamphey Palace

Remains of a palace of the bishops of St David's. The western wing dates from the thirteenth century, the eastern from the fourteenth.

Situation: 2 miles east of Pembroke. Map sheet 151, ref. SN 018009.

Llawhaden Castle

A fortified residence of the bishops of St David's. Earlier defences of timber and earth were replaced in the early fourteenth century by a stone curtain with projecting towers and hall.

Situation: 3 miles north-west of Narberth. Map sheet 151, ref. SN 073175.

Pentre Ifan Burial Chamber, Newport*
One of the finest burial chambers in Britain. The remains consist of a capstone supported by massive uprights. Outside the chamber proper was a forecourt.
Situation: 1½ miles south-east of Nevern. Map sheet 139, ref. SN 099370.

St David's, Bishop's Palace
Extensive remains of the principal residence of the bishop of St David's, built for the most part between 1280 and 1350. The richly ornamented arcaded parapets are the work of Bishop Gower (1327–47).
Situation: St David's. Map sheet 151, ref. SM 750254.

St David's, Close Wall*
An enclosure was in existence at least as early as 1172, the present walls belonging to a reconstruction of *c.* 1300. The enceinte was designed for the protection of the cathedral community and embraced the Bishop's Palace and canons' residences as well as the cathedral church itself.
Situation: Surrounding the cathedral close.
Admission: The wall is visible at many points; there is no access to the wall top.

St David's, St Non's Chapel*
The chapel, dedicated to St Non, mother of St David, is a single compartment structure measuring approximately 40 ft by 20 ft. Only the lower part of the walls survives. The south end, composed of dry-built walling of very large stones, may be of pre-Conquest date, the remainder being a reconstruction of the later medieval period.
Situation: ¾ mile south of St David's. Map sheet 151, ref. SM 752243.

St Dogmael's Abbey*
Ruins of the abbey of St Mary the Virgin founded for monks of the reformed Benedictine Order of Tiron in 1115.
Situation: 1 mile west of Cardigan. Map sheet 139, ref. SN 163458.

Index

Abbey Cwmhir (or Cwm-hir), 97
Aberconwy, 98
Aberdare, hut group, 45
Aberdaron, Myndd Rhiw, 8
Abergavenny, 33, 61
   priory, 63
   Roman fort, 33
Abergwili, 91
Aberleiniog, 59
Aberystwyth Castle, 66, 70, 80, 81
Avebury, 24

Bangor, friary, 99
   priory, 49
Barclodiad y Gawres, burial
   chamber, 20, 21, 114
Bardsey Island, 65
Basingwerk Abbey, 63, 92, 95, 96,
   98, 99, 122
Beaumaris Castle, 68, 80, 82, 83,
   114
Beddgelert, 65
Bere Castle, 80
Blaenavon, iron works, 101
Blaen Rhondda, hut group, 45
Bodowyr, burial chamber, 104
Brecon, 61
   castle, 83
   friary, 99
   priory, 98
Brecon Gaer, 33, 34, 35, 40, 117
Breidden, hill fort, 54
Bristol, 73
Bronllys Castle, 76, 117
Bryn Celli Ddu, burial chamber, 19,
   20, 21, 22, 114
Bryntail, leadmine, 102, 124, 129
Builth Castle, 66, 80, 81
Bulwarks Camp, Chepstow, 27, 29
Burrium (see Usk)
Burry Holms, 50

Cae Gaer, 41
Caer'hun, 33
Caer Lêb, 114
Caerleon, 32, 33, 34, 35, 38, 40, 41,
   43
   amphitheatre, 40, 127
   Prysg Field, 38, 40, 127
Caernarvon, 59, 65
   castle, 59, 68, 70, 80, 82, 83, 86,
   89, 98, 118
   Segontium, 33, 118
      town walls, 69, 82, 118

Caerphilly Castle, 79, 122
Caersws, 33, 35, 45
Caerwent, 29, 35, 36, 44, 127
   Pound Lane, 44
   temple, 44
   town walls, 36, 44
Caer y Tŵr, 27, 115
Caldicot Castle, 76
   Roman kilns, 44
Capel Garmon, burial chamber, 12,
   14, 120
Capel Lligwy, 115
Cardiff, 40, 61
   castle, 35, 73, 75
   friary, 99
   priory, 97
   Roman fort, 40, 44
Cardigan Castle, 66
Carew Castle, 86
Carew Cross, 52, 130
Carmarthen, 35, 45, 54, 66
   castle, 66, 85
   priory, 63, 96
   Roman sites, 35, 45
Carreg Cennen Castle, 66, 85, 120
Castell Bryn-gwyn, earthwork, 24,
   25, 115
Castell Coch, 123
Castell Collen, 34, 35, 38
Castell y Bere, 65, 68, 126
Chepstow, 44, 58, 60, 61
   Bulwarks Camp, 27
   castle, 75, 78, 83, 86, 127
   Port Wall, 127
Chester, 32, 40, 42, 60, 66, 73, 80
Chirk Castle, 80, 82
   gates, 120
Cilgerran Castle, 73, 78, 82, 83, 130
Clegyr Boia, Neolithic settlement,
   10
Clifford Castle, 58
Clynnog Fawr, oratory, 49, 50
Clywedog, 102
Coelbren, 41
Coity Castle, 75, 124
Conwy, 66
   castle, 68, 80, 82, 83, 86, 118
   town walls, 69, 118
Coygan Camp, 45
Craig Lwyd, axe factory, 8
Criccieth Castle, 78, 80, 83, 85, 119
Cwmbrwyn, Roman site, 45
Cwmhir Abbey, 97
Cymmer Abbey, 91, 96, 126

Degannwy Castle, 52, 59, 66
Denbigh Castle, 80, 82, 121
    Leicester's Church, 121
    friary, 121
    St Hilary's Chapel, 121
    town wall, 121
Derwen, churchyard cross, 121
Dinas Emrys, 55
Dinas Powis, 55
Din Dryfol, burial chamber, 16, 115
Din Lligwy, settlement, 46, 115
Dinorben, hill fort, 46, 55
Dinorwic Quarry, 103
Diserth, cross, 52
Dolaucothi, Roman mines, 42
Dolbadarn Castle, 65, 68, 76, 119
Dolforwyn Castle, 65, 130
Dolwyddelan Castle, 68, 75, 80, 119
Dovey Furnace, 101
Dyffryn, burial chamber, 18, 126

Eliseg's Pillar, 52, 53, 122
Elliot Colliery, 102
Ewenny Priory, 63, 91, 92, 95, 97,
    99, 124
Ewloe Castle, 76, 122
Ewyas Harold Castle, 58

Flint Castle, 66, 80, 81, 89, 122
Ffynnon Gybi, 50, 119
Forden Gaer, 34, 35
Furnace, 100

Garn Boduan, enclosure, 55
Garn Fadryn, 55
Gelligaer (or Gelli-gaer), Roman
    fort, 32, 34, 35, 36
Gloucester, 73
Glyntawe, cave, 45
Goat's Hole, Paviland, 7
Goldcliffe Priory, 63
Great Orme, Roman mine, 42
Grosmont Castle, 78, 128
Gwydir Uchaf, chapel, 119

Harlech Castle, 68, 70, 80, 82, 85,
    86, 126
Hawarden Castle, 80
Haverfordwest, priory, 63
Hen Gwrt, 128
Hereford, 60, 61, 73
Hirfynydd, Roman fort, 41
Holt, castle, 80, 98
    Roman kilns, 33
Holyhead, Caer Gybi, 115

Holyhead Mountain, hut circles, 28,
    46, 115
Holywell, St Winifred's Well, 50,
    122
Hope Castle, 80

Kanovium, 33
Kidwelly, 61, 63, 85, 120
    castle, 79, 120
    town gate, 120

Lamphey Palace, 90, 91, 130
Laugharne Castle, 45, 72
Leucarum (see Loughor)
Leintwardine, Roman fort, 34, 35
Llanafan Fawr, church site, 49
Llanberis, Dinorwic Quarry, 102
Llandegai henges, 8, 24, 26
Llandovery, Roman site, 33
Llandrindod Wells, Roman camps,
    34, 41
Llandudno, Roman mine, 42
Llandudoch (see St Dogmael's)
Llanfrynach, Roman villa, 44
Llangadog, Llys Brychan, 45
Llangar Church, 126
Llangenydd Priory, 63
Llanidloes, 102
Llanmelin Wood Camps, 27, 28, 29,
    128
Llanrhaeadr ym Mochnant, cross,
    52
Llanstephan Castle, 120
Llanthony Priory, 63, 95, 96, 97,
    128
Llantwit Major, church, 49
    crosses, 51
    Roman villa, 44
Llanymynech, 42
Llawhaden Castle, 73, 90, 91, 130
Lleyn, Tre'r Ceiri, 46
Llyn Peris, 102
Llys Brychan, Roman site, 45
Longtown Castle, 76
Loughor Castle, 124
Lydney, Roman villa, 36

Machen, Roman mine, 42
Maen Achwyfan, 52, 122
Maen Madoc, 49
Malpas, Roman site, 33
Margam Abbey, 63, 91, 95, 97, 98
Margam Stones Museum, 47, 48, 49
Mathrafal, 53

Monmouth, 58, 61, 63
    castle, 85, 128
    Great Castle House, 128
Montgomery, 59, 66
    castle, 72, 78, 80, 130
Mordunum (see Carmarthen)
Mynydd Rhiw, 8

Neath, 40, 41, 61
    Abbey, 63, 72, 91, 92, 93, 95, 96,
        98, 99, 124
    Gatehouse, 97, 124
Newcastle, Bridgend, 75, 123
Newgrange, 19
Newport Castle, 128
Newton Nottage, Neolithic site, 10
New Tredegar, 102
North Wales Quarrying Museum,
    104

Offa's Dyke, 57
Ogmore Castle, 52, 75, 85, 125
Old Beaupre Castle, 125
Oswestry, 80
Oxwich Castle, 72, 86

Pant y Saer, hut group, 56
Parc le Breos, burial chamber, 12,
    13, 125
Paviland Cave, 7
Pembroke, 60, 61
    castle, 63, 71, 72, 76, 78, 83, 86
Penally, cross, 52
Penarth Fawr, 119
Penarth Head, Roman site, 36
Pen Llystyn, Roman site, 41
Penmaen (Glam.), burial chamber,
    12
Penmaen-mawr, Craig Lwyd, 8
Penmon, 49
    cross, 49, 51, 116
    dovecote, 116
    priory, 49, 65, 93, 95, 116
    St Seiriol's well, 49, 50, 116
Penrhos Feilw, standing stones, 24,
    116
Penrhos Lligwy, 115
Pentre Ifan, burial chamber, 16, 131
Penygwryd, Roman camp, 32
Penylan Hill, Cardiff, 7
Pillar of Eliseg, 52, 53, 122
Plas Cadnant, fort, 55, 56
Plynlimmon Mountains, 41, 59
Port Dinorwic, 104
Portmadoc, 105

Presaddfed, burial chamber, 16, 116
Pumpsaint, Dolaucothi, 42
Pwllheli, 65

Raglan Castle, 72, 75, 85, 86, 89,
    129
Reculver, Roman fort, 35
Rhuddlan, 61
    castle, 66, 75, 80, 81, 82, 83, 89,
        122
    Twthill, 73, 122
Runston Chapel, 129
Ruthin Castle, 80

St Briavel's Castle, 80
St Cybi's Church, Holyhead, 36
St Cybi's Well, 50
St David's, Bishop's Palace, 89, 90,
    96, 131
    Cathedral, 49
    Clegyr Boia, 10
    close wall, 131
    St Non's Chapel, 50, 131
St Dogmael's, 49, 51
    Abbey, 63, 91, 92, 95, 96, 98, 99,
        131
St Donats, Roman site, 44
St Fagan's Folk Museum, 104
St Lythan's, burial chamber, 12, 13,
    125
St Non's Chapel, 50
St Seiriol's Well, 50
St Winifred's Well, 50, 122
Segontium, 33, 34, 35, 36, 38, 40,
    46, 118
Shrewsbury, 80, 73
Skenfrith Castle, 73, 76, 78, 129
Stonehenge, 21, 24
Strata Florida Abbey, 51, 72, 92,
    93, 95, 97, 99, 119
Swansea Castle, 90, 125

Talley Abbey, 91, 97, 98, 120
Tamworth, 56
Tenby Castle, 83
Tinkinswood, burial chamber, 12,
    125
Tintagel, 49
Tintern Abbey, 63, 91, 92, 93, 95,
    96, 98, 129
Tomen y Mur, 34, 41
Trecastle Mountain, Y Pigwyn, 32
Trefignath, burial chamber, 16, 116
Tregwehelydd, standing stone, 24,
    117

Tremadoc, Roman site, 45
Tre'r Ceiri, hill-fort, 46
Tretower Castle, 73, 75, 76, 117
    Court, 118
Tŷ-mawr, standing stone, 24, 27, 117
Tŷ-newydd, burial chamber, 117

Usk, Roman fort, 30

Valle Crucis Abbey, 52, 92, 95, 96, 98, 99, 122
Venta Silurum (see Caerwent)

Wantyn Dyke, 56

Welshpool, Roman site, 45
Wentwood, 28
Weobley Castle, 126
White Castle, 78, 79, 129
Whitland Abbey, 72, 91
Whitton Crossroads, Roman villa, 44
Wigmore Castle, 58
Wroxeter, Roman town, 34, 42, 45, 53
Wyndcliff, Roman site, 44

Ynys Seiriol, hermitage, 50
Y Pigwn, Roman camps, 32
Ystradfellte, Roman camp, 32
Ystrad Rhondda, hut group, 45

This series of Regional Guides to Ancient Monuments maintained by the Department of the Environment is planned to cover England, Scotland and Wales.

Other volumes available

1 NORTHERN ENGLAND 30p (33½p)

2 SOUTHERN ENGLAND 45p (50½p)

3 EAST ANGLIA AND THE MIDLANDS 55p (60½p)

5 SCOTLAND 50p (58½p)

6 CASTLES 25p (30½p)

7 ABBEYS 40p (45½p)

8 SCOTTISH CASTLES 27½p (33p)

9 SCOTTISH ABBEYS 60p (67½p)

   Prices in parenthesis include postage